AF398900

The Gift of Abhyasa

a personal encounter with the yogic trinity

By
Ansgar Schoeberl ©

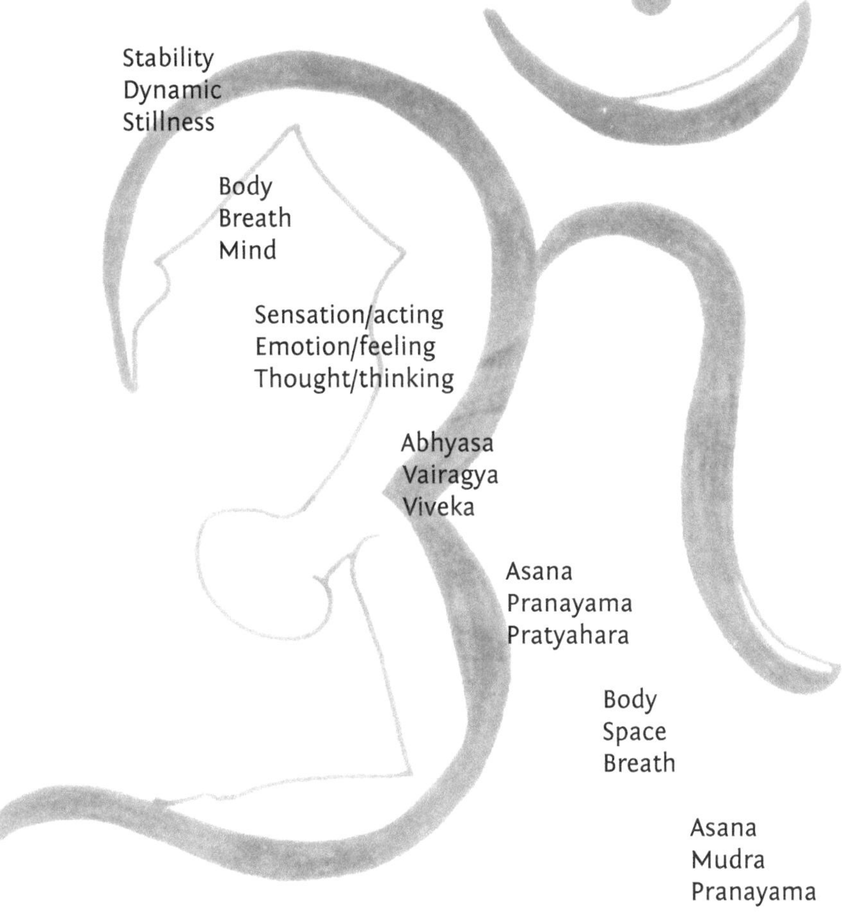

© 2013 Ansgar Schoeberl
Manufactured and published by
BoD - Books on Demand, Norderstedt, Germany
ISBN 9783848267217

To my Parents
&
Teachers

Foreword

These texts came through between 2003-08 as part of a intensive practice period, and I used them so far as a textbook for the workshops. My gratitude goes especially to Max, Nicole and Gal who have helped a great deal at that time to get it into shape.

Now, thanks to the professional and friendly help of Saleema, here on the beautiful island of La Palma, we formated it into a booklet ready for publishing.

It is not a general work on Yoga but a specific text for a particular approach through personal practice. To investigate into, experiment with, and understand that, which can be investigated, experienced and understood – the person. Personal understanding versus ideal imitation which is the hidden factor behind many yogic styles.

I revised the texts several times to make them more accessible, but I was cautious not to dilute the content in favour of easy reading. The many fotos serve for the coffee table-book aspect to lighten up the density of the content.

I did not add a glossary as I tried to be careful with sanskrit terms and used only those (explained through context) which I deem important for practical yogic philosophy and which are almost impossible to translate without loosening part of their meaning. So I left them in their original purity, either to be remembered or forgotten.

Certainly it is not a book to propagate or argue for Yoga but to inspire those on the free path of personal practice. Some chapters may be difficult to deal with and there is a need for patience and goodwill on part of the reader. Anyway, if inspite of that they fail to inspire and ignite curiosity, there is no reason to hang on to, but better to put or throw them away. So much said, here it comes …

La Palma, Feb. 2013   Ansgar Schoeberl

BOOK I
METAPHYSICS

BOOK II
PHYSICS

ASANA: Sthira, Sukham & Ananta-Samapatti

MUDRA: Bandha, Kriya & Ujjaya

PRANAYAMA: Puraka, Kumbhaka & Rechaka

BOOK III
TRANSPHYSICS

ABHYASA OF PRATYAHARA

VAIRAGYA OF NI-YAMA

VIVEKA OF SAMYAMA

APPENDIXES:

Introduction

At some moment in our yogic journey, after having spent time practising the various invented and patented Yoga systems developed by individuals and institutions, promising and certifying the wonderland of yogic names and forms, there might arise an inner urge to rediscover the origins of our practice. To discover that source from where the various systems and techniques have emerged.

»I believe that every student of Yoga should not only read but actually study the Yoga Sutras. It is an excellent way of delving into the metaphysics and the spiritual practice of Yoga. All too often, western students want to bypass the philosophical aspect of Yoga and get on with its practice. But it is impossible to practice Yoga authentically without first having grasped its metaphysics. Conversly, Yoga metaphysics will not reveal its full depth to someone who stays aloof from the practical disciplines. …
The Yoga Sutras offer a wonderfull oppurtunity to expose oneself to the condensed wisdom of centuries of spiritual experimentation and to allow one of the great adepts of that tradition to inspire one's personal practice of Yoga.«
- G. Feuerstein; ›The Yoga Sutras of Patanjali‹, p.7/8 -

Yoga, never aiming at becoming a systematic tradition or institution, defines itself through the personal experience and understanding of its practitioners. It is a living testimony of inspired and free-minded seekers who are motivated by an inner urge and curiosity for Self-exploration and understanding without relying on promises and expectations. Learning through teachers and teachings to trust in ourselves, we are reconfirmed by our own practical experiences. Such a yogic lineage sustains itself through individual dedication and living example, rather than through tradition and hierarchy. Quite contrarily the wisdom coming from understood Yoga practice is a conducted lifestyle based *on inner maturity, instead on outer authority!* It should eventually free us from institution and authority and enable us to live according to our own truth, naturally and harmless. »Yoga is to be known by Yoga. Yoga is the teacher of Yoga. The power of Yoga manifests through Yoga alone. He who does not become careless, negligent or inattentive, he alone rests in Yoga and enjoys Yoga» (as is stated by Vyasa, the mystical commentator of yogic and vedic lore).

From where does the desire arise to name and classify our Yoga practice, insisting on qualifying subtitles, when our nature and essence rests and reveals in and through Yoga itself? Is it expectancy caused by insecurity and lack of clarity regarding our personal understanding of Yoga and its path? Don't we trust in the natural potential of Self-motivated yogic practice? Or is it pointless obsession with certain styles and techniques, showing that we don't link to the bigger picture and stumble along between backaches, blocked nostrils, minute attempts of stillness and wishful thinking?
The objective of this text is to inquire into our threefold persona of *body, breath & mind,* our potential qualities of *stability, dynamic & stillness* and our personal traits of *sensation, emotion & thought.* By developing a personal practice of Asana, Pranayama & Pratyahara within their metaphysical context of Abhyasa, Vairagya & Viveka, we may understand our personality as it is and access the yogic maxim of Nirodha – the right cessation of wrong identity.
Because of the infinite variety of personal constellations and individual tendencies Yoga is abundant in possible ways to access the cultivation of its practice which is the common feature of all yogic endeavours. The practice of **Abhyasa** culminates into the intuitive understanding of **Viveka** which expresses in the right attitude of **Vairagya.** Thus the system in itself (or as it is) is Yoga and the numerous technical approaches offered are employed for cultivating a personal yogic practice: Abhyasa, the physical and personal link for the metaphysical and transpersonal truth of **Vairagya & Viveka** – refining, merging into and revealing each other.

»We hear today about different kinds of Yoga: Raja-Yoga, Hatha-Yoga, Jnana-Yoga, Laya-Yoga, Bhakti-Yoga and Karma-Yoga. These are all modern terms. They were not known to ancient Yogis and if some of them occur at all in old literature, their use is purely incidental and not indicative of a separate and exclusive technique. The standard text-book on Yoga, Patanjali's Yoga Sutra makes no mention of them. Certain aspects of the practice of Yoga have been needlessly apotheosized and elevated to the false dignity of separate sciences, without paying heed to their interrelations.«
- ›Philosophy of Gorakshnath‹; A.K. Banerjea Delhi 1988 -

Part 1

Life is defined through relationship which always has a complementary and controversial dual nature. Yoga as union always means the understood relationship of something relating to something. Relating to Yoga is the active attempt of fusing encountered paradigms into one understanding that transforms perceived diversity into unified perception. The complexity of theory dissolves in the simplicity of practice and as practice matures and complexifies it dissolves in the simplicity of the teachings. Complexity and simplicity follow and interact (being in relation) with each other in the pattern of the sinuscurve – simplicity complexifies and complexity simplifies ... simple complexity and complex simplicity – until they merge in personal integrity.

Philosophy is the reasonable domain of speculation which gets expounded in metaphysical theories and confirmed in physical practice. The use of yogic theory is to give us the right mental frame why and how to approach practice. We need a bit of theory to get a picture and lots of practice to fill it up; to correlate and reconfirm practical experience with expounded theory strengthens our conviction and gives faith. It lies in the self-revealing dynamic of Yoga that the experience encountered in practice contains and reveals the concept expounded in theory. Theory widens the scope for practice and our practice confirms the truth contained in the teaching. The physical insight we perceive in our practice, finds its counterpart in metaphysical comprehension and gives true conviction within and without.

In Yoga the emphasis is clearly on practice and not on a war of theories. Experimental understanding through personal practice instead imposed knowledge through imagined theory. Not to fall into the pit of philosophical complacency, neither to identify with the complacent kicks of rushing adrenalin or cerebral suppressions. We do get regularly acquainted with yoga-scholastics which are either fashionable simplified and turned into pop-art prose, or so heavily analyzed and academically complexified, that they manage to split the original and essential relationship between Yoga theory & practice and deprive it of any empirical personal access. A wise practice is *abhyasic* in its effort, *vairagyic* in its attitude and the resulting *vivekic* flashes of insight are highly inspiring when found and confirmed in the teachings and in daily life. Put in a nutshell it is in the *vivekic* transcendence of personal contradictions and conditionings where Yoga reveals itself. The key lies in the attitude *(Vairagya)* of how we approach and pursue our practice *(Abhyasa)* in particular and our life in general. *Yoga has no answer but dissolves the question.*

... freedom from the person & personal freedom ...

Freedom from the person means personal freedom from the false notion that we are confined within the limits of body, breath & mind. To be free from our personal claim means also to be free for personal unfoldment. We use *Asana* for freedom from the body and for bodily freedom; *Pranayama* for freedom from the breath (the vital body) and for vital/organic freedom; *Pratyahara* for freedom from the sensual mind (the mental body) and for mental freedom. Freedom happens through understanding and understanding brings freedom from false notions. Thus we use Asana to understand the body, Pranayama to understand the breath and Pratyahara to understand the sensual mind. Freedom *from and for* the selfclaimed identity of our personal re(du)ality. »This false identification is the cause of all man's ills. The means to terminate his suffering is by way of self-absorption, by withdrawing and demolishing all pseudo-identities, until the Self is ›excavated‹ from all the manifold layers of psycho-mental debris.«   - G. Feuerstein, Y.S. 1989, p.11-

Yogic practice is always a practice of *nirodha* or cessation in its respected field – the cessation of wrong identities and their limiting restrictions: The practice of *Asana* is the cultivation of asanic qualities within the *body* in order to cessate *sensational* identity and freedom for sensation.

The practice of *Pranayama* is the cultivation of pranayamic qualities within the *breath* in order to cessate *emotional* identity and freedom for emotion.

The practice of *Pratyahara* is the cultivation of pratyaharic qualities within the sense-objected *mind* in order to cessate *sensual* identity and freedom for the senses.

And in its higher practice Yoga turns into the cessation of personic identity in total through *Dhyana,* which is the yogic maxim of ›*chitta vritti nirodha*‹ (Y.S.1.2) and into complete freedom for personal expression.

Our personal choice and emphasis of practice varies due to individuality and environment; the empirical borderlines between body, breath & mind (from a practical as well as from a personal viewpoint) are really quite vague and from a wider perspective they merge, revealing diverse aspects of one integer whole. It is for the sake of our limited understanding that we divide them and give them a gradual ›step by step‹ appearance. In the actual experience they single, mingle and unfold in the always bigger picture.

A well performed Asana may bring one straight into the steady realm of onepointedness. Prolonged subtle and free breathing can immerse one into states of deep absorption and concentration. Mindful stillness naturally slips into meditation, while a strained effort for meditation is often nothing more than a poorly performed posture.

The compositional proportions of these techniques depend upon our individual capacity and need for personal experience. The cocktail which liberates one keeps the other in bondage as in the old story of medicine and poison. The art of measuring and mixing to make it positively potent wants to be discovered by ones own effort and expertise.

the ashtangic unfoldment

Yamas & Niyamas are the source as well as the destiny of the ashtangic process and the paths of **Bahiranga** and **Antaranga** are their respective means.

The path of **Asana** is the practice of **stability**, exposing and overcoming **sensational** distractions of the person – the **body** in the body.

The path of **Pranayama** is the practice of **dynamic**, exposing and overcoming **emotional** distractions of the person – the **breath** in the body.

The path of **Pratyahara** is the practice of **stillness**, exposing and overcoming **mental** distractions of the person – the **mind** in the body.

These three **angas** constitute **Bahiranga** or our personal practice of **Kriya-Yoga**. They weaken our neurotic afflictions and cultivate transpersonal experience and insight (Y.S.2.1-2). As the body holds the breath and gives space to the mind, so stability holds dynamic and gives place to stillness. The *gross* refines into the *fine* and merges into the *subtle. Sattvic* mental stillness is the personal harmonisation of *rajasic*-respirational dynamic and *tamasic*-bodily stability.

This refined still space of the mind is the elemental transition into all-pervading silence and in the transpersonal space of consciousness it is the domain of **Antaranga** *(Dharana, Dhyana, Samadhi).* Their combined path or *Samyama* is the practice of *prakritic* knowledge and *purushic* understanding. By truly understanding this ego-ic union with our person *(Samyoga),* we may dispel our ignorance *(Avidya)* with the discriminative knowledge of *Viveka,* which liberate us into the all-one-ness of the *Self.* Freedom isolated from bondage, which is *Kaivalya* (Y.S.2.17/23-26).

... the Practice of Ashtanga Yoga ...

The *attitudal* practice of *Ni-Yamas* is the passive unfoldment of **Vairagya.**

The *personal* practice of *Bahiranga* is the active unfoldment of **Abhyasa.**

The *transpersonal* practice of *Antaranga* is the potential unfoldment of **Viveka.**

Kriya Yoga

Kriya-yoga is the journey from *Samyoga* or the personal union with our ego-ic identity to *Yoga* or the freedom of Kaivalya, where the Self abides and shines in the all-one-ness of its glory – *the union between the Self and the Same.* The implied action of Kriya (from ›kri‹ – to do) is the dismantling of the person. It is a process of dis-identifying with the perpetuating layers of our personic being and their sensational, emotional & mental claim of our body, breath & mind. Kriya means letting go the insistence of being confined and limited into our personality. This happens externally through intense practice **(tapa),** internally through self-relation **(svadhyaya)** and intuitively through transcendence and understanding **(ishvarapranidhana)** – *impersonal development at personal risk.*

The practical experience of the infinite range within our finite personality might drive us to the limits of comprehension and make us wonder to whom all those experiences belong: Who is there when we step beyond our personal limitations? Who do we meet when we have rid ourselves temporarily from the burden of our personic identity? What is there when we translucify that misty space which qualifies the mind to be the source of ourselves? Where is then the personality and its idea of going beyond? In the total clarity of understood being we mingle and single within and without in all-pervading space, understanding the emptiness of illusive reality and the fullness of real illusion: the *ishwaric* experience – *from jiva to Shiva.*

>»M: Remember, you cannot abandon what you do not know.
> To go beyond yourself, you must know yourself.
> Q: What does it mean to know myself?
> By knowing myself what exactly do I come to know?
> M: All that you are not.
> Q: And not what I am?
> M: What you are, you already are. By knowing what you are not, you are free of it and
> remain in your own natural state. It all happens quite spontaneously and effortlessly.
> Q: And what do I discover?
> M: You discover that there is nothing to discover. You are what you are and that is all.
> Q: But ultimately what am I?
> M: The ultimate denial of all you are not.«
> - Nisargadatta Maharaj, ›I am That‹, p.24 -

... the Practice of Kriya Yoga ...

Tapas: the practice of **Abhyasa:** the *personal* practice of *Asana, Pranayama & Pratyahara.*

Svadhyaya: the practice of **Vairagya:** the unfolding *attitude* of *Yamas & Niyamas.*

Ishvarapranidhana: the practice of **Viveka:** the *transpersonal* maturity for *Dharana, Dhyana & Samadhi.*

The *ashtangic* pattern is a two-dimensional unfoldment, culminating in temporal *samadhic* states and stages and is the blueprint of successful yogic endeavour. The trinity of *Kriya* symbolises the three-dimensional expression of the whole or totality encompassed, culminating in *samadhic* cessation of our ignorance *(Avidya)* and hindrances *(Kleshas)* and showers the understood freedom of *Kaivalya* upon us.

Part 2

Inquiry into the known

»It is the ignorance of the known that creates the fear of the unknown.
It is the ignorance of the bondage that creates the illusion of freedom.«
- Vimala Thakar, ›Totality in essence‹, p.16 -

Body, breath & mind woven of the same cosmic fabric are stirred into life by pranic/gunatic motivation. They reveal our underlying personic patterns or *vrittis,* which have their source and destiny in the self-conscious totality of our person the *Chitta.* Into this organic/*pranic* interwoven web (body, breath & mind) we want to inquire and investigate: to understand, integrate and eventually let go of its limiting identity. The schism or duality which Yoga wants to transcend is not to be found between body and mind, matter and energy or the physical and the psychic. They are essentially formed from the same stuff, *Prakriti* or the worldground, constituting our tri-*gunatic* personality in gross, fine and subtle manifestations. The real and meaningful duality is to be found between our personality complex and that what makes us selfaware; between *Prakriti & Purusha.* To understand this primal duality, we need to experience deep and profoundly the compact unity of the ›known‹ *(Prakriti)* the empirical and personal. By truly understanding the known, the ›unknown‹ *(Purusha)* will reveal its Self; this is yogic inquiry or **Yoga-vichara.** The *vairagyic* attitude and *abhyasic* effort merge into a *vivekic* understanding of who we are not – body, breath & mind – but enable us to be, to express and to live out our indivi(sible)duality. *Abhyasa & Vairagya* represent the two wings on whose body our personal practice soars up to the heights of *Viveka.*
Dealing in *Bahiranga* with our personality and exposing it to be the tridal phenomena of *body, breath & mind,* which manifests in gross and subtle ways but always moving along the same gunatic-pattern of *stability, dynamic & stillnes,* symbolised through *Asana, Pranayama & Pratyahara.* Eventually this inner journey or involution towards the source of our Self opens to a ›higher‹ form of *Abhyasa,* the transpersonal practice of *Dharana, Dhyana & Samadhi* on the *Antaranga* level.

... stability, dynamic & stillness ...
or
Pratiprasava – involution through refinement & subtlefication –

From the stability of the body in Asana, via the dynamic of the breath in Pranayama, into the stillness of the mind in Pratyahara.

Asana is the *stable* opening of the body, its spinal *dynamic* and *still* alertness for enduring, persevering and merging into the pose. Pranayama is a *dynamic* opening on a respirational & pranic level: from the thoughtful breath of oxygenated air to the thought-free reception of pranic space. The *stability* of the inhale arouses the breath, the *dynamic* of the transition expands and subtlefies it and the *still* evenness of the exhale remerges the breath. The expansion (Prana-**ayama**) of the breath creates a spatial experience of Prana which needs an asanic body, which holds and not blows. The control (Prana-**yama**) of breath creates a spatial ability of specifically activating and working with the forces of Prana. The pranayamic *dynamic* within the *stability* of an asanic body merges into a sense-absorbed space of *stillness* in Pratyahara; it is a *still* opening on a mental or sense-ual level. The *stable* mental space, its sense-collected *dynamic* and its *still* endurance prepares for possible silent and cosmic mergings into the *silent space of spaceless silence* or the void of cosmic consciousness.

Grasping the code of our personality, this involutionary journey *(pratiprasava)* refines on the subtlest level of Abhyasa (Vairagya & Viveka), through the transpersonal practices of *Dharana, Dhyana & Samadhi.* Having refined the grossness of the physical body into the fineness of the respirational breath and into the subtleness of mental space, the subtlefication goes further on within. The dynamic of a stable breath in Asana, pulsating into pratyaharic stillness gives way to the *stability* of dharanic concentration, the *dynamic* of dhyanic meditation and the *stillness* of samadhic identity.

Likewise the core-space of our *Chitta* (personal totality) refines threefold as well: from our mental capacity of storing and activating memorial functions – **Manas,** via our notional need for self identity – **Ahamkara,** to our pure and intuitive intelligence – **Buddhi,** where it resembles the space of cosmic intelligence – *Mahat;* and eventually merges into the transcendental void of primordial matter – *Mula-Prakriti … refining and subtlefying the space of elemental Akasha into the void of nirvanic Shunya.*

As long as we are primarily preoccupied with the body we will do Asana to free ourselves from this preoccupation in order to prevent confusion of developing different and isolated techniques. We leave the actual decision up to *Abhyasa* which knows intuitively where to put emphasis in our practice.

Yoga-Vichara

Yoga-Vichara means practical inquiry into and understanding of the relative ›seen‹ or ›known‹ (Prakriti/Nature/Phenomena), instead of hypothetic speculation about the absolute ›seer‹ or ›unknown‹ (Purusha/Spirit/Noumena). And even though this absolute noumenal spirit is somehow inherently felt by everyone and is the ultimate driving-force in our life. It is through understanding the known that the unknown will reveal itself. *Right personal understanding leads to the perception beyond the person.*

Our individual expression is through our threefold personality and the universal expression is through the cosmic guna-tic trinity. *Body, breath & mind* with their fluctuate traits of *sensation, emotion & thought* discover, comprehend and complement each other through the gunatic qualities or values of *stability, dynamic & stillness.*

They are physically symbolized through *Asana, Pranayama & Pratyahara* and express metaphysically through *Abhyasa* the art of yogic practice, which refines into *Vairagya* the art of yogic attitude and *Viveka* the art of yogic insight. *It is always an encounter with the same tridal pattern, either within (individual) or without (universal).*

The nature of our person is ever changing being. Understanding our personality means not to identify with those changes and using our person in the best way we can. Most distractions we encounter in everyday life are less real than they are personal (mental, emotional or sensational) and cloud our perception of life as it is – and us as we are. The skill is to live with those distractions less identified. The beauty of Yoga practice lies in working with what we know to have – body, breath & mind – and not relying on external means or believe systems.

Part 3

Kaivalya, Prakriti & Purusha
... the free nature of the Self ...

>»It is often said that, like classical Samkhya, Patanjali's Yoga is a dualistic system, understood in terms of Purusha and Prakriti. Yet, I submit, Yoga scholarship has not clarified what ›dualistic‹ means or why Yoga had to be ›dualistic‹. Even in avowedly non-dualistic systems of thought such as advaita Vedanta we can find numerous examples of basically dualistic modes of description and explanation.«
> - Ian Whicher; ›Yoga the indian tradition‹ 2003, p.51/52 -

Yogic freedom or *Kaivalya* is the all-one-ness and pristine radiance of *Purusha,* our true nature or ›Self‹, untainted by *prakritic* identity. Patanjali expounds an absolute but also interdependent dualism between *Prakriti & Purusha.* He gives no chance to take refuge in the illusion that freedom could be reached at intellectually, neither that the final delusion could be reasoned away or to think ourselves free. Nothing like it, as the whole of our mental realm belongs to *Prakriti.* In order to understand this idea of an absolute non-dual yogic state or *Kaivalya,* we have to become intensely aware of the phenomenal nature within our personal identified world. If this phenomenal nature is not personally experienced and understood, we won't have the capacity to access the isolation and cessation process of *Nirodha* – from the identified to the non-identified state or the right cessation of wrong identity.

An understood letting go of habituated *prakritic* identity needs to happen and not only on a fragmental/conceptual but on a holistic/perceptual level. To cut the afflicted chain of *raga/dvesa* (clinging/aversion) and to stop our personal claim for ego-ic identity, there has to take place a profound recognition and transformation within. To realise and free ourselves from the tyranny of personal conditionings, patterns and concepts.

This may happen inexplicably, immeasurably, even unreasonably (and for sure uncertifiably) through the yogic path of *Abhyasa, Vairagya & Viveka.* Then the pure power or *chitshakti* of our true nature *(svarupa)* will start to shine forth and we can wholeheartedly let go of our neurotic will to do, control, master and steer. It lies in the essential nature of *Prakriti* to serve and reveal our *purushic* source and destiny, by refining the gross experience of *bhoga* into the subtle emancipation of *apavarga* (Y.S.2.18 & 21). *Freedom (moksha/apavarga) isolated (kaivalya) from bondage (klesha).*

Absolutely we rest in the all-one-ness of the Self *(Purusha)* enjoying and experiencing the playground of this world *or* the play of this worldground *(Prakriti)* and let life happen. And even so this doctrine of a *dvaitic* or dual philosophy might appear unattractive to ›armchair philosophy‹, it is a practical and physical expounding of a metaphysical path and not a speculative quest for mental satisfaction and complacency. *In the truth (satyam) of the practitioner (shivam) lies the real beauty (sundaram).*

>»The culmination of the Yoga system is found when, following from dharmamegha-samadhi, the mind and actions are freed from misidentification and affliction and one is no longer deluded or confused with regard to one's true form (svarupa) or intrinsic identity. At this stage of practice the yogin is disconnected (viyoga) from all patterns of action motivated by the ego. According to both Vyasa and the sixtennth-century commentator Vijnana Bhikshu, one to whom this high state of purification takes place is designated as a jivanmukta.« - ibid, p.59 -

>»Thus no one is bound, and certainly no one is liberated, nor does anyone really move through the cycle of rebirth; it is Prakriti alone in her many relations who is bound, who moves through cycles of birth and death and who is liberated.«
> - Samkhya Karika 32 -

Abhyasa
... dedicated abidance or the gift of practice ...

»As we have seen, Patanjali's most general statement on the nature of spiritual practice
is that it aims at the cessation (nirodha) of the various disturbances or ›turnings‹
(vrittis) of the mind (citta) through repeated practice (abhyasa) and dispassion
(vairagya). What is most striking about this formulation at least in the present context is
that the cessation of the activity of citta is said to derive from a form of activity.
Repeated practice, repetitive activity, leads beyond activity.
Thus the key to the cessation of action is action itself, properly carried out.«
- D. Carpenter, ›Yoga the indian tradition‹ 2003, p.35 -

Patanjali introduces *Abhyasa* as an continued and dedicated effort to stabilize oneself in
the cessation of ego-ic identity. It becomes established and firmly grounded when it has
been cultivated consistently for a long time with dedication and sincerity (Y.S. 1.12-14).
Abhyasa is that kind of practice where we ›abide in‹ and are ›engaged with‹ ... a meeting
with ourselves in the light of yogic practice. *Abhyasa* is not done for the sake of the technique itself, which constitutes the practice but for the sake of the unfolding attitude ar-
rounded. We practice Asana, (Mudra), Pranayama & Pratyahara so that we can abide
through them in the moment to moment awareness of abhyasic experience. *Abhyasa*
wants to be practiced with total involvement and integrity. *We practice the effort of
Abhyasa for a vairagyic attitude to emerge, and thus merging into vairagyic Abhyasa or
abhyasic Vairagya. The cultivation of right effort refines into right attitude.*

It is a constant encounter of our Self with the many layers and moods constituting our personality. It is a day-to-day meeting with our ever changing and fleeting mentality, reflected on the steady background of an abhyasic screen. Care has to be taken not to turn
Abhyasa into a rigid or self-righteous discipline leading nowhere except to expectation,
pride and the end of all wonder. The necessary motivation to abide in the moment to moment awareness of *Abhyasa* comes through natural curiosity or resonance and an awakening dormant energy in us which deeply wants to express herself. Strive and discipline
might be helpful in removing some lethargic layers covering this energy but not much
further. The actual touch is through wonder and surrender, with *Abhyasa* being our access
and expression – never repetitive but always fresh.
Abhyasa is an evolutionary and volitional method which grows and reveals through our
constant engagement with it, while the emerging detached attitude of *Vairagya* prevents
ego-ic identity and dependency with the techniques we use. *Abhyasa* is the active engagement and *Vairagya* the passive emergence truly reflecting our approach to practice in
particular and life in general. Non-striving and non-achieving it wants to be expressed for
the fulfilment of itself, non-expectant and self-content. *Abhyasa* is our volitional means for
yogic access, bringing about the yogic attitude of *Vairagya* and flowering in the clarity of
yogic insight, the discernment of *Viveka*. *From the push of external effort to the pull of internal unfoldment or from personal mastery to transpersonal understanding.*

Vairagya
... the inner unfoldment or emerging attitude ...

›Freedom of the senses from their objects (experienced or imagined) and eventually
freedom from any craving towards gunatic-phenomenal experience because of
knowledge of the noumenal (Purusha) are the signs of accomplished Vairagya‹
(Y.S.1.15-16).

The detached attitude of *Vairagya* unfolds internal and impersonal through our external
and personal abhyasic integration and assimilation of asanic, (mudric), pranayamic & pratyaharic qualities. Vairagya secures us from getting stuck or lost in the practice by keeping
the link to an always bigger picture in which all ego-ic effort seems pathetic. Abhyasa is
the active art of right practice and Vairagya is the passive art of right attitude. *Cultivating
a personal practice is the aim of Abhyasa and living a personal life is the gift of Vairagya.*

It is the incentive or motivation with which we take up the practice which will determine
our attitude and it is the attitude which expresses our real progress in practice. The real
incentive can't be a fancy or idyllic one. Many promises freely advertised by popular Yoga
for becoming a ›better‹ person and being more pure, calm, (w)healthy, happy, holy or successful might sound attractive but are actually wishful thinking and fantasy, partial and
estranged from our personal reality. This will not lead to integration but to attitudes which
are also partial and estranged.

The techniques employed should not be done for promised rewards but as means to understand the particular workings of our individual nature. And from here comes the true
incentive or motivation, because we want to find to out, because we want to understand
this personality we are living in and with. Who are we? Or rather, who are we not but
what makes us being? Those questions come from a space deep within and the urge to find
out also comes from there. Within and beyond the striving body, its stressing breath &
mental mind. ... *The mind is certainly not sincerely interested in those inquiries, since they
question its self-claimed originality.*

Viveka
... intuitive insights or discerning clarity ...

Abhyasa provides the foundation, Vairagya prevents it from becoming sidetracked and
Viveka gives clarity and understanding. Here in the heralding of *Viveka* is shown the true
potential of Abhyasa: from a metaphysical concept it reveals itself as a physical experience
of the dual and interpolar nature of our practice and personality. It is the gift of Abhyasa
that it links us to the higher spheres of Vairagya & Viveka. *The temporary stilling of the
mind through vairagyic Abhyasa becomes a lasting freedom from the mind through the vivekic insight of understanding and integration.* With Abhyasa & Vairagya we can still the
mind temporarily through *nirodhic* cessations, while with the arising third dimension of
Viveka we might lastingly cut the identificational claim of our mind-stuff *(vrittis)* and
abide in the natural clarity of true identity *(svarupa).*
This triad of *Abhyasa, Vairagya & Viveka* symbolizes in a whole the unfoldment of the
Kriya-yogic process (Y.S.2.1) and is particular to be found within every single limb and
technique we are engaged with. The effort of establishing Abhyasa in a vairagyic way culminating in vivekic insights and effortless abidance in Abhyasa ... *a natural perception of
life and reception of its grace.*

Nirodha
... right cessation of wrong identity ...

»Seen here, nirodha thus is not, as is often explained, an inward movement that annihilates or suppresses vrittis, thoughts, intentions or ideas (pratyaya), nor is it the nonexistence or absence of vritti; rather, nirodha involves a progressive unfoldment of perception (yogi-pratyaksha) that eventually reveals our true identity as Purusha. It is the affliction (klesha) evidenced in the mind and not the mind itself that is at issue.«
- Ian Whicher; › Yoga the indian tradition‹ 2003, p.53 -

Understanding and freeing the purushic Self from our identified prakritic personality cannot be done by annihilation, suppressive stopping or restrictive control, since the Self needs to be embodied in the person to be experienced and understood (Y.S.2.18-23); but it can be done by cessating attached identity with it (Y.S.1.2/3) which is the process of *Nirodha*. If the *Nirodha* of *Chitta's vrittis* would mean their annihilation (i.a. of right understanding, sleep and memory), we would have to destroy the mind itself and with it our personal capacity to survive in the phenomenal world (Prakriti), since all the *vrittis* (well or ill bred) are part and parcel of our expressed *Chitta* or consciousness. »The vrittis are the angas (parts) of the angin (whole) which is the chitta« knows Bhojraja in his commentary on the Yoga Sutras. Also if ›*chitta vritti nirodah*‹ would primarily mean the complete restriction or stopping of the vrittis, it would denote to temporary states into which we come in and out due to our restrictive effort. Thus it could not be a lasting freedom or resting place in our true nature or *svarupa*. The *Nirodha* of Chitta's vrittis defines Yoga and thus should at least be potentially a permanent state, where we can abide as free beings in this person and in this world.

This is why Patanjali gives interdependent reality to Prakriti (Y.S.2.21-23) and does not treat it as mere illusion or ›maya‹, where the position of the person would not matter or even exist because being illusive and conjured, (and there would be no meaning then in personal understanding and the nirodhic process).

Since it could be argued that *Nirodha* comes from the prefix ›ni‹ plus the root ›rudh‹, which means ›to restrain‹ more than ›to cessate‹, we could say that *the cessation of mental identifications brings with it a restriction of mental modifications.*

Nirodha is accessed through right practice (Abhyasa) with right attitude (Vairagya) as stated in Y.S.1.12. This results in the purification of our Chitta and expands the mind into a sattvic condition where it can seemingly (because even the sattvic mind with its pure and liberating concepts is a modification whose identity wants to be ultimately cessated) merge and unify with the Self. Repeated experiences of those practices leave a strong imprint on us and build up extraordinary faith, conviction, strength and insight (Y.S.1.20) which are necessary to prepare us for deeper plunges into the non-identity but interconnectedness between ›our Self & our person‹, *Abhyasa, Vairagya & Viveka* can be seen as the threefold expression of metaphysical *Kriya-Yoga* (Y.S.2.1) which reveals in physical practice through the pattern of *Ashtanga* and *Nirodha* is the yogic product during this process. It is the yogic relative to the vedantic principle of ›neti-neti‹, negating the transient to reveal the eternal. In both yogic & vedantic views it is Vairagya & Viveka which enable us to cross the threshold of the person. *It is the gift of Patanjali, that he gives us an actual access through Abhyasa.*

In buddhist teaching the third noble truth of ›duhkha nirodha‹ means the cessation of suffering not in the world as perceived, but for the individual due to right purification. The noble nirodhic truth of Patanjali does not mean the death of the mind through suppression and strain, but ending personal suffering through right cessation of wrong identity.

Nirodha is the dissolution of our personal claim and leads to a compassionate outlook of life, because experiencing the cessation of suffering wrong identity might well be the highest and humblest grace to live with in this phenomenal world.

Part 4

the one, the two & the three

»M: Only when spirit and matter come together consciousness is born.
Q: Are they one or two?
M: It depends on the words you use: they are one or two or three. On investigation
three becomes two and two becomes one. Take the simile of face – mirror –
image. Any two of them presuppose the third, which unites the two.
In Sadhana you see the three as two until you realize the two as one.«
- Nisargadatta Maharaj; ›I am That‹; p.458 -

One is the outer *access,* **two** is the inner *process* and **three** is the vital *progress/success.* In the phenomenal world it is the *trinity* which gives access to process *duality* and progress to *unity;* unfolding trinities, their dual minglings and unique mergings. The particular expresses through tridal patterns, unfolds in dual terms and unifies, once understood, into the whole – the one without a second … which is the third.
The personal phenomenon of dual experience merges into a transpersonal perception of the noumenal reality. Emphasis is given on tridal, dual and unified states and experiences, their interconnectedness and underlying sameness of ever recurring patterns. At the respective stages of our practice we will stumble again and again across those patterns, rediscovering and reconfirming their metaphysical value through physical experience. *Plurality moves via duality towards unity, which in turn expresses itself in tridal diversity.*

Abhyasa-Vairagya-Viveka – the yogic trinity
or
the outer access, the inner process & the vital progress/success

Abhyasa (practice)	effort	**Asana**	stability	**Body**
Vairagya (detachment)	letting go	**Pranayama**	dynamic	**Breath**
Viveka (insight)	balance	**Pratyahara**	stillness	**Mind**

From the stability of the body to the stillness of the mind via the dynamic of the breath.

From the physical to the psychological via the physiological.

From the stability of Asana to the stillness of Pratyahara via the dynamic of Pranayama.

From the stability of the body to the stillness of the breath via the dynamic of space.

From the stable body of Asana to the still breath of Pranayama via the dynamic space of Mudra.

From the stability of effort to the stillness of effortlessness via the dynamic of letting go.

From the stability of tama to the stillness of sattva via the dynamic of raja guna.

From the stability of Bahiranga to the stillness of Antaranga via the dynamic of (Ni-)Yama.

From the physical stability of Abhyasa to the metaphysical stillness of Viveka via the attitudal dynamic of Vairagya.

Establishing an engagement with ourself in the light of yogic practice

Asana	stability	**Body**	sensation
Pranayama	dynamic	**Breath**	emotion
Pratyahara	stillness	**Mind**	thought

With **Asana** we start to open the body, free the *breath* and reveal the *mind;* a journey commenced everything else follows. Linking movement with *breath,* we reclaim the *body* by opening it and free the *breath* by rediscovering it. Thus we give space and rest to the *mind* by keeping it engaged with *asanic body-breath* coordination. The technique of Asana is such, that in the beginning it is physically so demanding that breath & mind are absorbed within the bodily challenge. The physical challenge of Asana stretches un-needed sensations out and gives space to the *breath* to be less emotional and more vital. As the body opens and stabilizes, the attention moves towards the breath and its vital dynamic. The practice moves towards **Pranayama.** A vital *breath* in a stable *body* gives the sense of space needed for an open *mind* and the practice of **Pratyahara.** Here the sensually crowded *mind* opens and stabilizes in the sense of ›beingness‹. Thus as far as the person and its practice goes, one process leads to another while actually all happen simultaneously with shifting emphases ... as body, breath & mind are always happening together with changing personal emphases – the *stable* process of *opening* body, breath & mind into mobility, vitality & clarity.

Mudra
or
... from the ideal to the real ...

Actually the *mind* and its still practice of *Pratyahara* remains for a long time too subtle and evasive for direct personal and practical access. Until the body and its breath are practically understood through Asana and Pranayama, the mind will be a mere frictional expression, veiling and crowding the necessary stillness for Pratyahara.

Therefore we concentrate on the relationship of Body & Breath – Stability & Dynamic – Asana & Pranayama – Sensation & Emotion – Abhyasa & Vairagya. Their understood interplay and harmonisation unify into the potential for *pratyaharic mental stillness*, its *thought-free* space and revealing *vivekic* insights.

Body & Breath merge into their common place – **Space** (as the body needs the breath within and the breath needs the body without). In yogic practice this space is expressed through **Mudra** which gives stability to Asana and holds dynamic in Pranayama. A place where practical and personal integration can take space – *space is the place!!*

therefore we shift our Yoga-practice

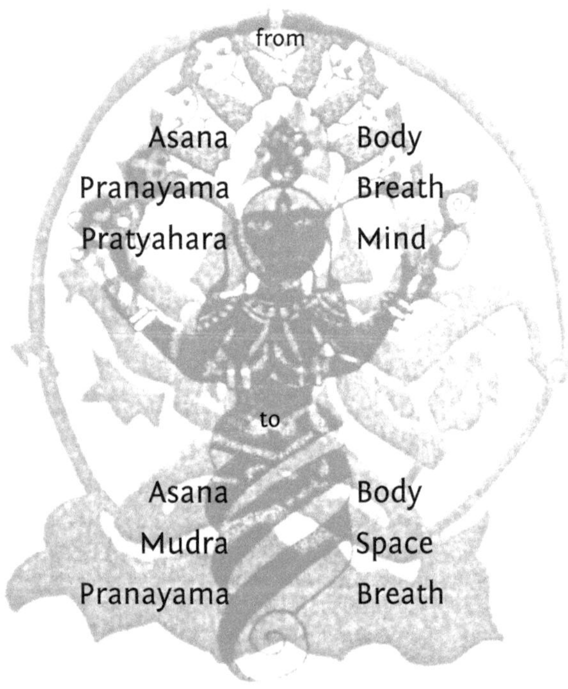

Thus our practice of **Yoga** always reflects and reveals the gunatic trinity of **stability, dynamic & stillness** (subtlefying or grossifying due to personal need) and actually consists of:

Asana:	Sthira	Sukha	Ananta-samapatti
Mudra:	Bandha	Kriya	Ujjaya
Pranayama:	Puraka	Kumbhaka	Rechaka

To give us a sense of metaphysical origination and physical access, Patanjali roots those principles right into the quality of **Asana** and thus gives us the gross direction from where to proceed: *Sthira, Sukha & Ananta-samapatti* via *Prayatna-shaitilyia* and potentially up to *Dvandva-anabhigata* (Y.S.2.46-48). This is surely not to empower Asana as a body cult but meant as a direct means to access the yogic pattern or process right from the gross aspect of the body and using it as a launching pad for the subtler spheres of our practice and person.

»Do not be satisfied with hearsay or with tradition or with legendary lore or with what
has come down in scriptures or with conjecture or with logical inference
or with weighing evidence or with liking for a view after pondering over it or with
someone else's ability or with the thought ›the monk is our teacher‹. When you know in
yourself: ›these things are wholesome, blameless, commended by the wise and
being adopted and put into effect, they lead to welfare and happiness,
then you should practice and abide in them.«
- Buddha (Kalama Sutta) -

»Disciple: Meditation is possible only with control of mind, which can be achieved only
through meditation. Is this not a vicious circle?
Bhagvan: They are interdependent; in fact meditation includes mind control, the subtle
watchfulness against intruding thoughts. In the beginning efforts for control are greater
than for actual meditation, but in due course meditation wins and becomes effortless.
D: Your grace is needed for it.
B: Practice is necessary, there is grace.«
- Teachings of Sri Ramana Maharshi -

ASANA

Sthira, Sukham & Ananta-samapatti ... in Asana

... assimilating asanic qualities into our personal practice ...

»There is no danger in practising Pranayama, Asana etc if you are careful
and if you use common sense. People are unnecessarily alarmed.
There is danger in everything if you are careless.«
- Sw. Sivananda -

»It is the body which is the instrument through which spiritual aims are achieved. This
is hatha yoga. The Natha statement is an uncompromising insistence on a spiritual
discipline. But the suggestions and viewpoints are very different from those of righteous
and enthusiastic practitioners of hatha yoga today who treat the asanas as a symbolic-
magic complex under a pseudo-scientific garb. It seems that the concept of Asanas as a
medium of exploration of the conscious and unconscious mind has been lost sight of.«
- ›The Yoga Tradition of the Mysore Palace‹; N.E. Sjoman '99, p.47 -

Part 1

The asanic potential lies in its capability to explore and experience our bodily totality, with
the capacity to make the body understand itself. A bodily analysis on a personal level. As
long as we have preferred or rejected postures, blank areas, places we cannot (or don't want
to) feel, sense or move, we are ignorant of their aspect within the body. To remove this ignorance we direct awareness through breath and flexibility through stretch to those spaces
and open them up. This is the discriminative *(Viveka)* aspect of our practice which comes
about by doing Asana *(Abhyasa)* in order to find out and understand the bodily aspect of
our persona without getting attached to it *(Vairagya)*. This detachment or Vairagya towards
wrong notions of success or failure in our practice (of *asanic* Abhyasa) prevents us from
injuries, pride and frustration. To open our physical *(sensational)* blocks in this way, follows
the same patterns as to open our physiological *(emotional)* ones in Pranayama and our
psychological *(mental)* ones in Pratyahara: the process of stable opening our personality.

... dynamic of Asana ...

The wide possible range within our Asana practice, from sitting still up to dynamic pos-
turing, lies in the very nature of dealing with the body. As soon as the historic yogic shift
happened from defining Asana as ›being the seat we are seated upon‹ to the ›posing body
being the seat‹, all postural possibilities were potentially embraced. It lies in the very nature
of Asana that once we embark on its journey, we are bound to discover and integrate all

kinds of experiences, aspects and emphasises of the body through our dedicated and sustained engagement with it ... *nothing new under the skin but the infinite range within our finite structure.* Thus the means to understand Asana lies not in its sophistication as a postural system, even so it might be a symptomatic consequence of it, but in the emphatic shift to define Asana from being a ›place to be seated upon‹, to Asana being a ›bodily posture and attitude‹. This shift in the principle meaning of Asana opened a new dimension to investigate the bodily pattern of our personic matrix. It is this asanic evaluation inside the ashtangic integration and kriya-ic unfoldment, which gives us a very potent oppurtunity to link our modern Asana practice to the ancient yogic teachings, if we are willing and able to let the depth of Asana penetrate us. The self-generating dynamic of asanic inquiry will then become active and take us from the body via space to the breath and mind and eventually beyond the personal realm ... from Asana via Mudra to Pranayama and through Pratyahara into the silence of unitive absorptions ... *Dvandva-anabhighata in the Asana of Asamprajnata (Y.S.2.47 & 1.18).*

Due to lack of conviction, commitment and contentment we defend, criticize or judge Asana, where there is nothing to be defended, criticized or judged. It lies in the perfect nature of Asana that it ranges and unfolds in all its diversity from stability to stillness via dynamic. Actually Asana, Pranayama & Pratyahara symbolise the same personal process in gradual stages of refinement. *From the gross physical body via the fine vital body to the subtle mental body ... and beyond.*

Concerning ourselves with the gross aspect of our person we open, strengthen and ease the body. Then we can breathe into our finer aspects: opening, lengthening and subtlefying the breath, creating a functional harmonious space for the vital body. Being in harmony with our physical and organic realm, we merge into the subtle level of our personal complex, the mental body – opening, calming and emptying it.

This self-revealing and evolving pattern of involution is rooted in the natural process of personal investigation. We follow it, not because of traditional obedience but out of a natural curiousity resulting from personal practice and yogic inquiry *– from outer authority to inner maturity.* As long as we are unclear about the underlying unity and sameness of refining personal practice, we better stay with Asana until it refines itself and us.

The landmark or touchstone whether we perform Asana in a yogic way is the degree of emerging detachment. The closer we get to asanic accomplishment, the more the attachment (the desire which needs to be there initially to ignite and maintain motivation) will recede, until we can achieve the good pose without clinging. As the body opens, the space and breath become more interesting and relevant and then we are in the right space to practice in a pure and yogic way. Asana are not to be done in the spirit of achieving but of exploring and understanding; achievement and mastery are their byproduct. *The difference between basic and advanced Asana vanishes as our practical and personal attitude matures.*

... Sthira, Sukha, Ananta-Samapatti ...

In the practice of Asana (Y.S.2.46-48) there is a constant encounter with the triad of effort, letting-go & balance. The effort of stretching into the pose, the letting-go of settling into it (through loosening the initial effort or *prayatna shaitiliya)* and the balance or insight of abiding in *sthira sukham asanam* (at ease in a steady pose). Thus we assume Asana for certain periods, enduring but not strained and inwardly moving towards the mindful alertness and stillness necessary for *ananta-samapatti.* Patanjali uses the term *ananta-samapatti* (mental stability in infinity or the mind infinitely stabilized) and thus puts this asanic quality into the samadhic context whose principle is found as *samapatti* in Y.S. 1.41. Asana encompasses the steadiness of *sthira,* the ease of *sukha* and the mindfulness of *ananta-samapatti.*

This triad becomes obvious on the bodily level as stretching, settling and holding the body within its posture. It shifts on to the respirational level as inhaling, transitioning and exhaling rhythmical breath within asanic balance. Eventually this pattern reveals the mental plane where we observe the struggling and expectant mind with its desire to steer, achieve and become and transform it into the mindful one which let's go, settles and surrenders into the harmonious balance of body & breath.

The process from approaching to accomplishing Asana is thus an ashtangic process in itself, refining according to our abhyasic capacity and quality (as the process from Asana to Samadhi itself is internal and invisible to the naked eye). It is an ongoing experience and resolvement of our inner oppositional and therefore also complementary forces of *effort & letting-go* into *balance & transcendence*. The art to acknowledge and the insight to understand those forces help us in the process of resolving and transcending their impact on us. As B.K.S. Iyengar says, »the conjunction of effort, concentration and balance in Asana forces us to live intensely in the present moment«. *The purification of the body through Asana is actually a return to its natural and anxious free state where it can express itself through innocent postures and movements.*

»Through the rhythmic and harmonious relationship with the inertia (sthiti)
principle in Asana and the principle of motion in Pranayama, comes a purification of
the physical organism, helping the sustenance of pure perception
and the suspension of mental movement.« - Vimala Thakar -

... & Dvandva anabhigata ...

In Y.S.2.48 Patanjali states that the right application and accomplishment of Asana results in the ›unassailability‹ or *anabhigata* of the ›pair of opposites‹ or *dvandvas,* which means these *dvandvas* loose their impact on us in their whole range of wavering moods and modes. To disassociate from this dual grip, Asana wants to be *sthira*/steady, *sukha*/at ease and the initial effort/*prayatna* to perform, needs to be loosened/*(shaitiliya);* and most significant there needs to be *ananta-samapatti,* a cognitive absorption/*samapatti* of *ananta*/the infinite principle (Y.S.2.46-47).

By ascribing the transcendence of the *dvandvic* quest to Asana, Patanjali does not devaluate the classical philosophical importance of *dvandva*(and its need to be transcended), but what he does is to evaluate the practical impact and importance of Asana, by lifting it potentially/integrally up onto a samadhic level. *It is the gift of Patanjali that he links this dual transcendence from its speculative and theoretical heights, to the physical and practical access of Asana ... the right personal pose.*

According to Vyasas ›Yogabhashya‹ 2.32 (the first and foremost commentary on the Y.S.), *Tapa* is ›the patient endurance or resistance of the pair of opposites‹. *Asana as embodied Tapa.* And a little further in 2.52 it is commented that ›there is no Tapa greater than Pranayama‹ ... *asanic Pranayama or a dynamic breath in a stable body.*

All personal unfoldment start with the body and all yogic unfoldment start with Asana. By assimilating asanic qualities, we unravel the threefold pattern of our embodied person: posing – breathing – being or acting – feeling – thinking. As Karl Baier says »Asana is a bodily opening towards the wholeness of the world we live in«. To open the body skillfully gives space naturally to the breath. Breathing skillfully gives space naturally to the mind. Being still naturally – voila this is where our imagination ends and Yoga begins. *It is a gradual involution of evolution ... a revolution.*

... hips, shoulders & spine – the structural trinity ...

The existential and essential axis in our body is the *spine*. It is the first embryonic structure evolving from the navel cord and steadily unfolding two-directional into the whole fetus. It is the vital-vibrant core structure which initiates and adjusts to all possible bodily movements and postures. The *spine* absolutely needs the open stability of *hips & shoulders* to freely express itself and to be secured by their established foundation and ceiling – bottom & top.

In Asana we use legs and arms as levers to access and open *hips & shoulders*. To touch and awaken the vital space of the trunk along the spine-line. Roughly speaking, the further the outer levers (legs & arms) reach, the deeper is their inner access within the trunk; for example long arms stretch back and short shoulder blades lever forward to open chest and upper back.

The visible process in Asana is done by legs and arms and makes itself noticed in the stable opening of *hips & shoulders*. The invisible process is the spinal unfoldment through breath and space; the moment we actually feel the *spine* itself, we are likely on the way to injury.

... vinyasa & the cycle of circles ...

Thus it becomes obvious that the essential work is to open hips & shoulders, to unwind and free the spine, within the context of stability which Asana stands for. The body can do postures while *standing, sitting or lying*. It can move *forward, sideward, revolved, inverted and backward*. The revolve or twist is actually a combination of forward and sideward; as inversion and backward are continued extensions of forward. Therefore it is *forward* (vertical) & *sideward* (lateral) only which combine, extend and make up for the various directions. Understanding and following them we end up in Asana ... standing, sitting or lying.

– Open *hips* stand for the *stability* aspect and are accessed and opened effectively through standing, forward, sideward and revolved poses ... *the liquidity of the hips.*
– Open *shoulders* stand for the *dynamic* aspect and are accessed and opened best through inversions and back bends ... *the range of the shoulders.*
– Open *spine* stands for the *stillness* aspect and is accessed and opened passively (via hips & shoulders); actively it expresses its freedom as having space in every position, (specially in extended vertical directions) ... *moving forward, trusting back – expanding into the spine-line.*

The integration of these aspects and their understood interplay initiate the cycles in which the body moves in its individual circular range. Along those *cycles of circles* are found all the respective Asanas within personal reach and their smooth procedure make for the sequences known as *Vinyasa*.

THE YOGIC MUSCLE

The yogic attitude within the bodily challenge is one of enduring instead of achieving. To remain and breathe in the pose empowers the muscles to evenly and thoroughly stretch and develop their whole length. This gives stability without blocking flexibility. Muscles build up through an energetic transformation of heat during contraction. The common concept of muscle development is to single out particular muscle-groups and successively contracting and releasing them, mostly with the help of weights. This results in a visible muscle-bulk in a relatively short time but all the muscular process takes place in its centre, as there is no time for the energetic action to spread and extend over the whole length of the muscle from origin to insertion. That is the price for quick results, a bulky centre with weak attachments of origin and insertion; a visible local strength which connects invisibly weak with the whole of the body. Every quickly repeated strenuous and mechanical action leads to this phenomenon.

The idea of the yogic muscle lies in its total involvement from origin to insertion imbedded in a holistic action of the body. Abiding and enduring in Asana finding stability, balance and ease, gives time to evenly develop and build-up the muscular aspect. It is a harmonious interplay between acting, contra-acting and releasing, giving the body time and space to strengthen and endure stamina. With such a yogic muscle we can deeply penetrate into our bodily layers and get a direct personal (instead of academic) insight into our organic-muscular and structural-skeletal system. Developing, investigating and understanding our body through direct practical perception awakens a cellular intelligence within which goes beyond our physical and conditioned limitations and is metaphysical, unconditioned and boundless.

The key to understand the muscular body is direct experience through empirical personal practice, rather than studying it through referred anatomic theory. Thus we understand and resolve the (seemingly contradictory) patterns of:

> – Strengthening & releasing into endurance.
> – Stretching & releasing into endurance.
> – Opening & releasing into endurance
> – Effort & letting go into abidance.

Too much strengthening is powering and creates contracted local muscle bulk, which literally takes away the space and flexability to open and connect to the body as a whole. Too much stretching becomes bending and creates over-flexibility or hyper-mobility, leading to instability (the prosaic loosening of the backbone) and the inability for enduring and breathing through.
Too much muscular development gives rise to injury because we suppress our maturity to accept limits, overpower and break. Too much ›bendy‹ mobility gives rise to injury because we don't have the stamina and strength to hold our limits, over-bend and break. *Overdoing one aspect means underdoing another!*

The means to develop and balance both sides of the scale (stability & mobility) smoothly and well measured is our breath. The quality of the breath shows our yogic development in Asana (and other practices as well). The body represents the ›abhyasic‹ principle of steady and dedicated effort and its breath represents the ›vairagyic‹ principle of right attitude through letting go of external achievements and turn inward.

Thus the yogic muscle is evenly developed from origin to insertion. Its strength lies in the dynamic of accepting and enduring seemingly difficult situations and breathing through. *The yogic muscle keeps its strength and beauty for it & Self.*

Part 2

»The concept of Asana is a physical posture in which one is at total ease and in perfect
harmony with oneself. This has to be understood properly. As Patanjali and other yogis
referred only to Asanas which are static or which are used for meditation, many people
believe that the other Asanas, in which the body does not remain still, are not part of
this classification. Many people have classified Asanas as either non-traditional dynamic postures or traditional static postures, but actually Asanas cannot be classified in
this way. A much broader range is encompassed.«
- ›Yoga Darshan‹; B.S.Y.; p.137 -

It will take personal time until Asana reveals itself and it will reveal less through outer perfection than through inner understanding of how the body relates to and is able to assimilate asanic qualities. How do we involve the body and its parts in the stable process of
opening through alignment, elongation and expansion and from where arises the coordination for all these actions?

The sequential pattern to prepare, abide and come out of the pose should be part and
parcel within each Asana by experiencing the respective specialness, wholeness and com-
pleteness of each mo(ve)ment. Otherwise it might create a schism between ›less‹ and
›more‹ important poses, between bodily exercise and yogic practice and will then demand
continuous shifting between warming up, being in, coming out, countering and moving
on, distracting us from the unicity of the one body abiding in various postural circum-
stances. This would also serve the old mental pattern of striving for something new, ac-
quiring it and fluctuating onto the next … being busy creating instead of being the
creation. Those sequential and integral aspects are supposed to happen within every
Asana we assume, rather than the sum of assumed Asana. Repetitive performance of asanic exercises is not necessarily yogic practice and does not guarantee us the acceptance
of the inner body of what the outer does. The outcome of such practice can manifest in
symptoms such as:

... the body refuses to open in spite of long term efforts.
... we stretch for fear of stiffness and greed for flexibility instead of understanding and in
    corporating available asanic qualities into our bodily structure.
... we miss the interaction between coordinated muscle-stretch and joint-opening.
... we don't get the link between Asana, Mudra and Pranayama and treat them as inde
    pendent or even unrelated practices.
... we don't see an attitudal transformation through our practice. In short, we miss the
yogic point while doing yogic practice. Yet the power of bodily practice is such that we still
experience certain fitness and happiness.

Where are we in our practice? How much maturity do we need for asanic self-guidance
and further yogic practice? Can we reach that inner space teaching us where and how to
proceed along Asana? Are we incorporating a holistic range of Asanas or are we rejecting
certain aspects and cling to others? Can we accept the whole of our practice or are we preoccupied with special likes and dislikes? Are we able to contact the whole of the body during its practice? Are we aware of our idiosyncrasies or do we excuse them with fixed
routines? Do we understand how Asana move and penetrate the body? Do we let Asana
assume us or do we push the body into Asana? *Are we assimilating asanic qualities into
our body or do we want to control Asana through bodily posture?*

We come to know through the insights of understood practice. As long as we are overly
attached in either a positive or a negative sense Asana is not mastered; a mastered Asana
gives joy to perform including the effort but does not create an undue sense of attachment.

Once we persistently endure the steady opening of the body we tap into its innate intelligence, which will rightly answer all these questions (by doing away with them), given the case we are willing to listen. The body will give us signs when we are overly attached and also when we fearfully reject. The body will let us know about our individual limits and potentials, which usually lay beyond those we thought of.
The personal link between us and our practice requires, more likely than not, a teacher. The right teacher with the right teachings at the right time; to shift our practice from an acquired system of bodily practice to an unfolding bodily inquiry, revealing the personic patterns ingrained in our physics. From outside both practices might look similar, while from inside one is driven by an expectation to steer it into the most rewarding direction, while the other is motivated by an attitude of unfolding and understanding. Understanding the practice by letting it unfold into unknown and sometimes unexpected directions, finding the reward in each happening mo(ve)ment refining into the next.

There are many teachers and books around Asana and some are good and supportive. They help us to understand the outer form and the inner unfoldment. They show us how to choose, approach and join Asana to integrate our whole bodily range. Any amount of time and energy spent with books, teachers and systems is well justified if they guide us to this understanding and personal practice. ›Light on Yoga‹ by B.K.S. Iyengar might still be the most comprehensive book to get an exhaustive overview of Asana and after a few years we do get a grip of how to arrange, approach and select Asana without getting confused by the compact multitude of them. Our part is to be receptive to the teachings and enthusiastic to the practice with trust and patience.

As it is said in the Jyotsna commentary of the Hatha Yoga Pradipika (H.Y.P.1.17), »though it is impossible to explain clearly and realise the important truths that underlie the various Asanas, till the human system is understood in all its intricacy and detail, still it can be said that the various postures bring about many important results, physically and otherwise.« And this is what Asana is truly about, to holistically understand physically and metaphysically our bodily pattern. To realise our obstructing blockages and ›scorching‹ them away with the light and heat of understood practice.

Then the sometimes so little valued body in spirituality becomes a major key in actual practice to unlock the hidden chambers of our persona unveiling archetypes and patterns which normally remain buried away under layers of egoic fancy, fantasy and fear.

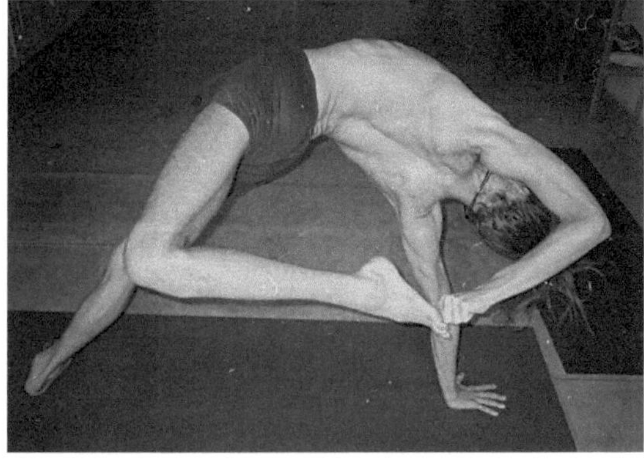

ON STAGES AND AWARENESS
Being in Asana:

Opening & aligning … stability of the body
Elongating & expanding … dynamic of the breath
Receiving & merging … stillness of the mind

While establishing our Asana practice it will be helpful to develop the following qualities until the body is open and the mind free enough to be moved by the breathing maturity of asanic understanding and self-guidance, which postures the body due to its need. There are four stages with corresponding awareness to perform Asana skill- and artfully. They happen of course simultaneous and are basically inter-woven, -mingled and -connected but for body's sake want to be approached in the following ›order‹, otherwise we might stagnate, frustrate and break down instead of free. They are inspired by the Asana teachings of Brahmarcharya Rudra-dev Gowda of Rishikesh, as understood by the author.

* OPENING … reclaiming the body
The body (most likely) needs to regain its birthright of flexibility, suppleness and subtleness, so that we can freely make use of it, instead of being used by its habituated and conditioned patterns. We reclaim our body through stretching and holding it. This will have deep and penetrating effects but is still happening on a fairly body-mechanic level. Unless the arising flexibility is integrally understood, the inner or cellular intelligence remains covered up and cannot be tapped to open the body from inside out. Getting stuck on this level is relatively easy if we blindly or for too long follow the promised security of set systems, telling us how to proceed. Much more we want to understand and open that inner space and maturity which frees us from those constricted and contracted habits of our body its breath & mind. *We want to stretch out of concepts not into them.* We can become quite bendy and gymnastic but if the inner link is missing, we might also break or become overflexible in due time and loose the grounding of the backbone and its associated metaphors. *The corresponding awareness is the ›bodily awareness‹, an awareness of the surface or touch of the body. … a getting into the pose.*

* ALIGNING … setting the base
Once we have reclaimed our bodies through stretch, we move further in towards the skeletal structure and its alignment. This is a shift from partial awareness which comes from flexibility to integral awareness arising from structural alignment. *Hips, shoulders & spine – the structural trinity:* A practical and effective way to check our alignment is to focus on hips & shoulders and by doing so we will realize with time and attention that these two major joints incorporate the whole body and are the base and firmament of the spine our vital axis or microcosmic *meru-danda*. We create a link between feet & hips via the knees, and between hands & shoulders via the elbows. This enables us to move out of the hips and out of the shoulders instead from somewhere in the lower or upper back. The legs give the link to open the hips and the arms give the link to open the shoulders, while

the knees and elbows are key-joints for access and success. Thus the spine will have the experience to open to its natural state, safely embedded between hips & shoulders; if we originate our movements from there the spine feels secure, trusts, opens and follows the direction indicated. While if not we bend the spine itself, overloading the vertebras by breaking/pushing out of the discs which are fairly limited in range, tearing and pulling the spine along its muscles and thus creating an unfair amount of pressure on the spinal structure (including nerves and brain extension) suffocating and harming ourselves. *The spine is sacred – not meant to bend – only to follow.* Alignment is totally essential to create an individual and intuitive body awareness and connection. It is the most important tool we can develop and without it we only get disturbed trying to proceed. *The corresponding awareness is the ›structural awareness‹, an awareness of placing the bodily structure ... a sett(l)ing into the pose.*

*ELONGATING ... creating space

Alignment is adjusting an open body within its structure, while elongation unwinds the body from within its spinal core. The open and set body is compulsory for the spine to unfold freely and it is this unfolding through elongation, that (re)awakens our breath and spinal space in ever wavelike and expanding motions. This awakening triggers, releases and unwinds our contracted habitual patterns – *from the fascia to the mind.* Since the spine is the archaic structure out of which the rest of the body emerged, it is here that each initiating dynamic takes place. Around the navel is the place where we all began, where each breath and move originates with a two-directional notion. With the initial moment of each breath we can catch this spinal elongation and tap into its cosmic rhythm – the rhythm that everybody and everything is part of. This initial mo(ve)ment goes down the lower lumbar and sacral spine into the legs and through the feet into the earth grounding and rooting us; while simultaneously it goes up into the thoracic spine fulfilling the chest and through the cervical spine up the neck and head into the sky and space above and around, making us receptive and inspired.

With inhalation we can sense and feel this two-directional elongation (from the level of the navel) and with exhalation we can become aware of its space and maintaining it; from ›opening & contracting‹ to ›elongating & maintaining‹ and eventually to ›elongating & expanding‹. Elongation is the pranic link which bridges our individual space within with universal space without – space is the place! *The corresponding awareness is the spacious ›mindful awareness‹, an awareness that links inner and outer, breath and move, place and space. ... a moving within the pose or spacing the place.*

*EXPANDING ... going beyond

We are open, aligned, elongated, at ease and home in the body. Well connected with the space inside and around us, riding the spinal wave of our personal rhythm: inhale & exhale. Now we are going even beyond this rhythm and into the source itself, by merging with it, becoming it and being the ocean itself. Letting go of letting go by *being the happening and happening in being.* Momentarily we can expand into that space where body, breath & mind merge.

Backbends, especially in combination with inversions and arm-balances are the last group of Asana to be introduced in our ›systematic‹ and therefore very relative Asana-evolution. To do them efficiently requires a mastery or internalisation up to elongation. Then we may expand beyond our imagined limitations and merge into the infinite range of our finite body. Our picture of the world is very much defined by our physical structure. We stand with the feet on the ground, head up and looking forward. With backbends and inversions we leave and reverse this conception, bringing the back to the front and the down- to the upside. Unfolding through spinal elongation, we expand and uncurl in spiral (more than linear) motions, widening and lengthening our dimensional range.

By now the body is so awakened that every move originates out of its spinal-core, running and vibrating in wave-like motions through the whole body and giving a much wider and longer range of movement than local attempts of pushing and pulling here and there. The spine turns into a liquid-solid wave and instead of doing the stretch or pose we are becoming it, becoming the wave – with each breath more solid, more liquid, more wave, more space. *The corresponding awareness is the ›limitless awareness‹; an awareness of dropping the limited mind into limitless expansion.*

SUKHASANA

Sukhasana, usually translated as the easy cross-legged posture, denotes to that natural and matured state of Asana which we want to access, experience and assimilate within every posture: *Sukha* the giver of ease & joy. Depending on each individual Asana this quality expresses itself in various ways and is clearly felt and evident once we experience it. In *Sukhasana* we are steady and content – ›sthira sukham asanam‹ – with all bodily distractions and contradictions overcome. The structural body rests in its alignment and so do the vital breath and mental space. We abide in the stability of the body, the dynamic of the breath and the stillness of the mind. Then body & breath are open, spacious and freely breathing to the cosmic rhythm of an awakened spine. The mind accepts the bodily posture, stops reasoning, analysing and doubting and releases a sense of contentment as far as the pose goes. Non-questioning and non-qualifying the mind is calm and stays unidentified with uninvited mental activities going on in its background.

Sukhasana is thus not the easy ability of assuming a pose but the ability of being at ease while in it – the art of abidance. After the necessary initial effort is loosened and the posture is bodily achieved, we might find ourselves in a personal balance with the body firm, the breath smooth and the mind expanding towards infinity. What happens when bodily contra(di)ctions are overcome and our personal(real)ity remains undistracted for the time being? With nothing to do and nowhere to go, we ›endure‹ *Sukhasana* with its unbearable ease of beingness and joy unclaimed.

The more elaborate and systematic the postural system is, either in complexity or in simplicity, the more chances we have to busy ourselves with those well developed concepts and miss the asanic event of being with and hanging out in the person: *where body, breath & mind happen to be and so are we … with the ease & joy of sukha.* To achieve this state of firm and content ease, we need to understand Asana thoroughly and therefore we must practice! With the number of yogic postures equal to the number of living beings or estimated 8400000, it seems more meaningful to accomplish Asana by going for its quality rather than quantity. Allowing Asana to consume the body and allowing the body to assimilate Asana, rather than pushing one into the other.

Asana ranges from the effort of *prayatna, via* its loosening of *shaitilya,* to the non-dual state of *dvandva-anabhighata,* via *sthira, sukham & ananta-samapatti;* or from the personal to the transpersonal via body, breath & mind. To assimilate those asanic qualities as expounded in Y. S. 2.46-48, is the self-fulfilling path of Asana in Yoga with *Sukhasana* becoming a practical expression.

The holistic and interdependent nature in the path of Ashtanga is such that each anga or limb contains the whole and the whole is contained in each anga. Every limb undergoes an ashtangic process in its practice. Asana (body) leads to Pranayama (breath), to Pratyahara (mind) and beyond, as well as containing them. Along the asanic path we experience all kinds of postures to discover, explore and understand this body. Starting with seemingly simple ones, we move towards the more complex and thus discover the bodily range in its totality. We reach out to its far corners and experiencing the infinite range within our finite structure, stretching, elongating and expanding into the beyond. Touching that space where the body merges with the breath in the mind. This merging is *Sukhasana.*

Thus in performing Asana, we extend our bodily experience beyond our physical conception, to truly experience the totality of the one (body) in all (body, breath & mind) and all in one. We check out our body in order to see it as what it is: the infinite variety of personal experience. Nothing new under the skin and nothing special to be found apart from a convicted personal truth that might put our striving mind at rest; *right here within body, breath & mind, at ease and anxious free we will find Sukhasana.*

... conclusion ...

We want to avoid the splitting of Asana into successive steps but stay with that flow where one move leads to the next, letting the inherent qualities unfold from within instead of superimposing them. The difference is an attitudal and therefore yogic one. If we stay in the wholistic spirit of Asana, we can prepare and counter as much as we like, as they are integral aspects of the same thing unfolding – the body. With this attitude we are likely to discover that all those aspects of preparing, abiding, coming out, countering and moving on are happening quite natural and spontaneously within asanic integrity and maturity. Most poses, if needed, counter and realign themselves by returning into the *samasthiti/* even stability of standing, sitting or lying and letting the breath take over. Some spontaneous wriggling here and there will release and unwind the body, keeping it sensitive, aligned and balanced. *Body with its breath & mind knows in which ways to move once we are awakened to it.*

... & transition ...

At this stage our Asana practice will reveal itself and each misconception or proud notion we follow will eventually come to light and bring us back to purity. Still working with a teacher from time to time will correct, inspire and enrich our own creativity which is fine as long as we don't fall prey to the ›yoga-class-attitude‹. *The real practice is a private event!*

Concerning the preparation and readiness for Pranayama, arm balancings and backbends open and strengthen the chest/shoulder area most efficiently, giving space and security to lungs and heart and can be indicators for our asanic maturity and pranayamic readiness. Asana & Pranayama could be reduced to either Asana as a refined cultivation of *stability,* or to Pranayama as a refined cultivation of *dynamic* (as stability holds dynamic and dynamic enables stability). Does the body carry and contain the breath or does the breath enable the body?

H.Y.P I.67-69: »Success comes to him who is engaged in practice. How can one get success without practice; for by merely reading books on Yoga one can never get success. Success cannot be attained by adopting a particular dress. It cannot be gained by telling tales. Practice alone is the means to success. This is true, there is no doubt. Asanas, the various Kumbhakas and the excellent Karanas (positions such as Mahamudra) are all in the course of Hatha Yoga to be practiced, until the fruit of Raja Yoga is obtained.«

»Some of the subsidiary results of practising Asanas are: ... development of willpower. The physical body is directly and in some mysterious manner related to the atma, the source for spiritual power. Gaining control over the physical body which mastery of Asana implies brings about an extraordinary influx of that spiritual force which expresses itself in outer life as will-power.«
- I.K. Taimni, ›Science of Yoga‹ on Y.S. II.48 -

PRACTICE

The general process in Asana is the *stability* of bodily positioning, the *dynamic* of the breath which lengthens and refines and the stillness of the mind which endures and merges. The specific process in the body is the stable opening of the hips (through standings, forward & sideward), the dynamic opening of the shoulders (through inversions and backward) and the still opening of the spine (through space and breath); this is of course to be done in the bigger context of stability for which the body stands for.

Such an opening exposes and frees us from our habitual bodily bonds and enables our natural *move-ability* or freedom of movement, which varies outwardly due to individuality but inwardly has the same personal process underlying. The weightless feeling of an elongating spine and the free unfoldment of the breath are the guidelines for asanic stretch.

It is this understood interplay of *hips, shoulders & spine*, which initiate the movements of the body in Vinyasa and it is through Vinyasa that this interplay becomes better understood and assimilated. Thus we place the body in one of its basic positions (standing, sitting, lying) and guide it through pronunciation of one of its directions (forward, sideward, revolved, backward, inversed) through the cycle of its individual capability. Along these cycles or circles manifest the various Asanas.

The spine symbolizes the vertical direction for forward, inversed and backward:
Tadasana – Uttanasana – Adho Mukha Vrikshasana – Urdhva Dhanurasana – Tadasana.

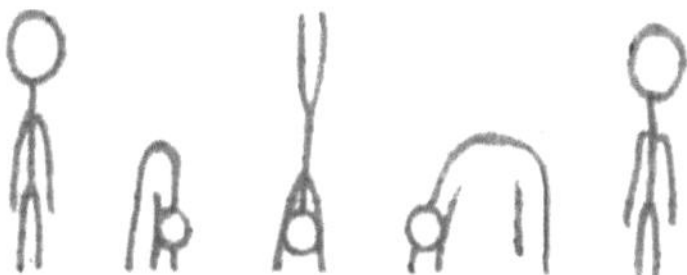

Vinyasa: Tadasana – Uttanasana – Adho Mukha Vrikshasana – Chaturanga Dandasana – Urdhva Mukha Shvanasana – Chaturanga Dandasana – Adho Mukha Shvanasana – Parshvatonasana – Virabadhrasana2 – Virabadhrasana3 – Eka Pada Uttanasana – Anjeyasana1+2 – Chaturanga Dandasana – Urdhva Mukha Shvanasana – Chaturanga Dandasana – Adho Mukha Shvanasana – Uttanasana – Tadasana – (change sides).

Hips & shoulders symbolize the lateral direction for sideward: Tadasana – Prasarita
Tadasana – Trikonasana – Ardha Chandrasana – Parshvakonasana – Virabadhrasana1 –
Prasarita Tadasana – Tadasana.

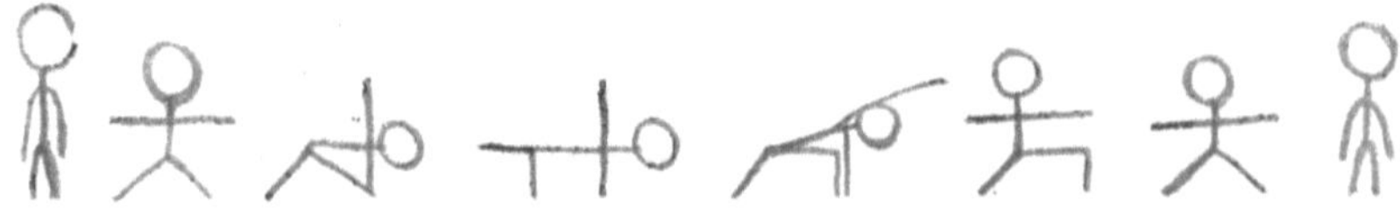

Vinyasa: Adho Mukha Shvanasana – Parshvatonasana – Trikonasana – Parshva Tadasana
– Virabadhrasana1 – Parshva Virabadhrasana1 – Ardha Chandrasana – Parshvakonasana –
Anjeyasana1+2 – Chaturanga Dandasana – Urdhva Mukha Shvanasana – Chaturanga
Dandasana – Adho Mukha Shvanasana – (change sides).

The revolve or *twist* symbolizes the different positioning of hips & shoulders, i.e. the for-
ward-positioning of the hips and the sideward-positioning of the shoulders or vice versa.
It is a combination of forward and sideward, as inversed and backward are extensions of
forward. Therefore the two principal directions are *forward (vertical) & sideward (lateral).*

The asanic multitude happens through the countless combinations of the *vertical* (spine) and the *lateral* (hips & shoulders) directions and the positioning of the limbs (legs & arms).

Standing: Adho Mukha Shvanasana – Parshvatonasana – Trikonasana – Parivritta Trikonasana – Prasarita Tadasana – Virabadhrasana1 – Parshva Virabadhrasana1 – Ardha Chandrasana – Parshvakonasana – Virabadhrasana2 – Parivritta Parshvakonasana – Virabadhrasana2b – Anjeyasana2 – Chaturanga Dandasana – Urdhva Mukha Shvanasana – Chaturanga Dandasana – Adho Mukha Shvanasana – (change sides).

Sitting: Adho Mukha Shvanasana – Trianga Eka Mukha Pada Pashimotasana – Eka Pada Navasana – Krounchasana – Eka Pada Shirshasana – Bharadvajasana – Ardha Badha Padma Pashimotasana – Janu Shirshasana – Eka Pada Navasana2 – Krounchasana2 – Eka Pada Shirshasana2 – Ardha Matsyendrasana – Gomukhasana – Lolasana – Baddhakonsana – Bakasana – Chaturanga Dandasana – Urdhva Mukha Shvanasana – Chaturanga Dandasana – Adho Mukha Shvanasana – (change sides).

Those examples show that in Vinyasa we give an impulse of direction and then let the body move through the respective cycles and circles of its individual capacity ... with minimal effort and maximal effect.Hypothetically we could say that those Asana which lie within our individual range of hips, shoulders & spine are basic and those Asana where we need an extended range of hips, shoulders & spine are advanced.

Mudra

Bandha, Kriya & Ujjaya ... in Asana

Bandha		Stability
Kriya		Dynamic
Ujjaya		Stillness

**Mudra gives stability to Asana and holds dynamic in Pranayama ... Space is the place.
The stability of Bandha holds the dynamic of Kriya and releases into the stillness of Ujjaya.**

»Asanas stabilize the body and enable Pranayama to proceed smoothly.
Through Pranayama the student tries to unite the prana & apana. Mudras seal this
union of prana-apana so that the union might not be disturbed. Bandhas lock this
marvelous effect. When the prana & apana are thus held in union, a great mysterious
and powerfull spiritual current is generated within, which cannot be described in
words and which has to be expirienced by each individual. This power pierces
the entrance to the shushumna. By Jalandhara bandha the prana is prevented
from flowing up and with Mula bandha the apana is prevented from flowing down«
- Sw. Vishnudevananda p.247 -

Part 1

Generally speaking Asana deals with the body (limbs), Pranayama with the breath (trunk)
and Pratyahara with the mind (head). As the trunk is the vital-*(organs)* and the structural-
(spine) centre of our body, it is natural that to give special emphasis here. This is where
Mudra *(Bandha, Kriya & Ujjaya)* comes in to prepare the trunk for pranic maturity. To
really comprehend the trunk as an open and accessible entity and learn its harmonious
interplay & -action, we need to understand the tendencies of its respective sections:
differentiating, developing and understanding them, we realize their structural integrity
as one vibrant dimension – *the vitality of our being.*

... the laws of personal unfoldment ...

Stable & open hips provide for a strong and safe foundation, where the pelvis can settle
into the basement of the pelvic girdle.
Stable & open shoulders provide for a wide ceiling, where the chest can freely expand in
the thoracic space of the shoulder girdle.
Stable & open breathing provides for a spacious unfolding of the spine, where the navel
is set in its abdominal centre.

Having opened the body with Asana, we now awaken and set the trunk with *Bandha &
Kriya* into its spacious nature for the free-flow of the breath in *Ujjaya*. This unfoldment
of the spinal space (pelvic, abdominal, thoracic) activated through Asana and empowered
by *Bandha & Kriya* releases *Ujjaya*. the established mode of vertical breathing.

The external workout via the limbs to open hips & shoulders makes space for the spine to set, unwind and elongate. The spine, our vital axis, is grounded and rooted down in the pelvic bowl and grows out of it like a tree spaciously embedded in its plot. This growing dynamic or ›spinal process‹ is internally triggered by *Mula-bandha,* empowered and maintained by *Nabhi-bandha,* amplified by *Uddhiyana-bandha* and reaching up to *Jalandhara-bandha.* It straightens, strengthens and lengthens our trunk. Upholding itself it gives stability, space and trust to awaken to the pranic unfoldment of Mudra & Pranayama: *from the structural setting of Asana to the pranic movement of Pranayama, via the set space of Mudra.*

The practice of **Mudra** turns the trunk into a sealed pot (kumbha) where the dynamic of Pranayama can merge into the stillness of Pratyahara. Here takes place the true *Kumbha mela* (festive ground) and here is the authentic *triveni* (or tridal meeting place) where *body & breath* confluence with the mystical *mind. Where the gross (body & breath) become subtle and the subtle (mind) become gross in the space of pranic transcendence.*

... the vital spaces & the dance of their shaktis ...

The trunk is divided into three main areas (which further subdivide once we explore into them), the pelvic-, the abdominal- and the thoracic- space. They are embedded in diaphragmic structures or qualities, which can extend up or down due to internal spatial need, with the *abdominal diaphragm* (separating the pelvic-abdominal and the thoracic space) being the largest and referred to if mentioned alone or as the *central* one.

The lower area, safely inside the bony structure of the hip girdle, contains the organs of procreation and excretion and is called the *pelvis.* It is the seat of *Mula-shakti* or the ›root-power‹, from where the deep seated originations of our individuality take place. Here is the cosmic source and trigger of original primal energy, vibrating our personal universe into being and pulsating through our spine into the brain.

The middle or central area, situated around the navel, is the space of the *abdomen.* It contains our digestive factory: receiving – breaking down – assimilating and sorting out bulks of food. It also contains our chemical laboratory: producing – storing – cleaning and detoxifying blood and other vital (plasmic) liquids. The abdomen is our physical-gravitational centre and the seat of *Agni-shakti,* which burns our digestive fire and empowers our vital process. She is the transformer of food into body through digestion and assimilation ... and on a subtler level she is the transformer of thought into ›me‹.

The upper area between the central diaphragm and the shoulder girdle is called the *thorax,* containing lungs and heart. These organs are so vital that they are protected inside the stabile structure of the ribcage, because it is their actions which define us being alive. The beat of the heart, pumping blood evenly througout the body, represents our integrity and individuality. The respirational action of the lungs show our need for relationships and interactions with our surrounding, through their constant (pranic & gaseous) exchange with the cosmic and atmospheric universe. It is the seat of *Prana-shakti* or the ›pure energy‹ which empowers us to witness ourselves.

Bottom and top of the trunk contain the openings for receiving, rejecting, excreting and ejecting. To turn the organic trunk into the pranic dimension of a *kumbha* (sealed pot), we need to prevent those openings from leaking ... *the space contained.*

The lower openings in the pelvic floor, the genital and anal orifices, can be isolated with *Vajroli* and *Aswini* mudras and are jointly sealed with *Mula-bandha* which works on the perineum between anus and sex; these actions mark the *pelvic diaphragm. Mula-bandha* triggers our spinal process physically and metaphysically it accesses our psychic reservoir situated at the *sacral* base of the spine, representing our karmic stock symbolized by the coiled up kundalini block. Mula-bandha loosens this block and redirects pranic energies into the central channel of *Shushumna nadi* the spinal canal.

The upper openings of the wind and food pipes (trachea and oseophagus) are closed off and checked by *Jalandhara-bandha,* the *lung-fulfilling* sealing touch within the throat, marking the *thoracic diaphragm.* Physically it unites chest and chin to prevent undue upsurges of gross energy into the head, while its subtle aspects refine through the neck into the cranium and brain. Metaphysically it unites the *prana* of the trunk with the *mana* of the head.

It is the vertical uplift through the *mula-bandhic* applied Ujjaya-breath which stimulates and binds the Bandhas efficiently. Bandha & Kriya set the stage for the free-flow of *Ujjaya* which then pierces and fuses all the three shaktis as *trishaktibedhana* into one vibrant vitality ... *prana moving & the dance of the shaktis.*

It is the *Uddhiyana-bandha* with which we amplify our natural sense of direction – to lift and shift up. Energizing *Agni-shakti* by pulling the navel in and sucking the abdominal contents back & up towards the central diaphragm and thus fanning her energetic flame high into the chest of *Prana-shakti.* This energetic momentum riding along the spine-line, *is lifting and shifting up towards finer and higher dimensions without loosing ones grounding.*

Physically this is indicated by the vertical spine which roots its short and sturdy lower part (lumbar) down towards the ground, while its longer and refining parts (thoracic & cervical) reach up and connect us to the above & around, giving us a sense of origin and direction.

This two-directional action of *rooting down and reaching up* takes place around the level of the navel, our physical and gravitational centre. The trunk gives the space, the digestive fire the energy & momentum and the spine the direction. *Our rajasic effort to lift up towards the sattvic realm of vibrancy instead of sagging down into tamasic sluggishness.*

Part 2

BANDHA, KRIYA & UJJAYA
or
moving into gravitational space

Mula Bandha
... triggering mula shakti ...

To contact *Mula-bandha,* which works on the contraction of the perineum (or perineal stripe) between sex and anus, we need first to contact, contract and single out Vajroli & Aswini mudras working on the pelvic floor of the genital & anal openings respectively. In Vajroli our focus is on the urethra and contracting it, we draw the genitals back and up. In Aswini our focus is on the rectum and contracting it, we draw the rectal vacuum back and up. The sheaths and layers of muscles and fasciae of the pelvic floor make for the perineal body, while the perineum in itself is the muscular stripe and tendon between anus and sex. Normally we are not aware of single functions here and contracting one (holding urine or stool) usually means contracting the other one as well. Practicing to hold them separately and learning to contract and relax them at will, gives us a feeling of their subtleness, connection and distinction and a certain control over the genital and rectal muscles.

The *Mula-bandha* works in the same way but is more subtle to reach and hold, as there is no external bodily function attached to it. Being able to perform Vajroli and Aswini, we concentrate on the perineum in between. Its access is the horizontal perineal stripe which wants to be contracted, sucked in and up, while the rest of the pelvic floor is kept as passive as possible. The contraction of *Mula-bandha* triggers the spinal process and *Mula-shakti* sets the pranic process free ... *from Mula-shakti via Agni-shakti to Prana-shakti* .

While it is already a challenging practice in itself to contact and hold *Mula-bandha* in static Asana, it is almost impossible to hold it for extended periods in dynamic Asana, since it requires too much attentive and concentrative energy. More often than not because of its subtle complexity, we loose the necessary finesse for access. and it is *Nabhi-bandha* which keeps the *Mula* cont(r)acted in dynamic performance.

Nabhi Bandha
... contacting agni shakti ...

The *Nabhi-bandha* is situated between Mula- and Uddhiyana-bandha at the level of the navel and integrates them two-directionally. It reaches down to Mula and spreads up to Uddhiyana keeping both connected and combines the energetic aspects of Mula & Uddhiyana during dynamic activity.
In *Nabhi-bandha* we use a slight contraction of the navel towards the spine, just enough to keep the abdominal tonus and our focal attention alert. As the Zen-master Sato Tsuji (cited from Graf Duerkheim) says, »if one tenses the abdominal muscles in the right way, there appears as a result of this tension, a point of concentration below the navel«; an abdominal friction to tone or tune the body into a state of dynamic vitality or vital alertness. The friction needed to stay engaged with life and not to drop off into the total relaxation of a corpse.

The *Nabhi-bandha* sucks our collected respiration into the navel and spreads it out in both directions along the spine-line. Extending down and elongating up, it roots us gravitationally and connects us anti-gravitationally. *Nabhi-bandha* keeps a respirational somatic link down to Mula and up to Uddhiyana and centres us in our middle.

Kapalabhati Kriya
... the firefanning Agnisaris ...

We strengthen our abdominal centre with the firefanning *(agnisaric)* Kriyas of *Kapalabhati 1,2&3.* They consist in contractive abdominal stimulations of the digestive fire to fan our slow burning vital furnace internally and to strengthen our physical centre, (belly) externally. This is done in combining abdominal contractions with active respirational(ess) emphasises. *Kapalabhati* belongs (together with Bhastrika) to the Kriya-family of *Agni* (fire) -*sari* (fanning).

Pushing and pulling the belly out and in with inhalation and exhalation is **Kapalabhati 1.**

Only pulling the belly in on the exhale, with the inhalation occurring passively, is **Kapalabhati 2**. Kapalabhati 1 & 2 can be done with both, single or alternate nostrils.

Abdominal *out-in* or vertical *up-down* contractive motions, while in external retention, are the two parts of **Kapalabhati 3.**

They do very efficiently increase the heat of *Agni-shakti,* strengthen the abdomen and bring an intense sense of awareness to our centre. Collecting our attention here, we can then volitional directed it because of the released pranic potential ... *either into asanic stability, pranayamic dynamic or pratyaharic stillness.*

Uddhiyana Bandha
... flying up ...

Uddhiyana is the ›flying-up‹ notion with which we shift our gravitational centre up to the higher abdomen, known as the solar plexus and also called the second brain. Here is the hidden chamber in which countless nerves of our autonomic system meet in a bundle *(kanda* or bulb), and spread out like rays of the sun. It is also the transitional place between abdomen and thorax, separated by the abdominal or central diaphragm. Both the abdomen and the thorax float in between fairly flexible ranges of parachute-like diaphragms. This allows the abdomen to contact down into the pelvis and reach up into the thorax, and it allows the thorax to contact down into the abdomen and reach up into the cervical region of the neck.

The abdominal space is secured by a deep layered network of criss-crossing muscle sheaths, fasciae and other connective tissue.
The thoracic space is secured by the bony structure of the ribcage and strong muscle sheaths in the back.

Uddhiyana-bandha develops and connects the transit area between belly and chest (guts and heart). It is best practiced in the standing pose of *Uddhiyanabandhasana* and once it becomes familiar and understood it can be done in firm sittings and various other static Asana. The full *Uddhiyana-bandha* with its intense back & up suction of the abdominal contents is quite a challenge and a practice in itself. It limits her full performance for a long time to voided moments of external retention (and should be introduced otherwise gradually and carefully); *otherwise the pranic link of Uddhiyana is held by Nabhi-bandha, which also binds the Mula.*

Metaphysically *Uddhiyana* is the ›take-off‹ which catapults the pranic process (after having been triggered and stirred by *Mula & Nabhi)* up our psychic channel *Shushumna* along and within the spine-line. This pranic process originates in the triangular sacral area and steadily refines from the broad lumbar, via the long thoracic, through the fine cervical spine into the ›thousand petaled crown-chakra‹ and the ethereal aperture of *brahmarandhra* at the top of the head, spreading out as cosmic rays of expansion and reception.

The process of *Uddhiyana* is two-fold. First it consists of fanning the digestive fire through a backward pull of the navel and then raising the abdominal pranic entities as high as possible into the solar plexus, moving with the concave-vacual sucking motion of the central diaphragm, and flaring up into the chest. Once it becomes relatively established and we can hold it for a while without respirational strain, we integrate Uddhiyana into bandhic Asana and take it over into the pranayamic process.

The *uddhiyanic* action symbolises and indicates the anti-gravitational directional up-shift towards the higher and lighter. ... *from the lower gravitational pull of personal conditionings to the higher antigravitaional expansion of transpersonal truth.*

Nauli Kriya
... churning the abdominal ocean ...

With *Bandhas* we contacted, contracted and released pranic force from the perineum via the navel to the solar plexus and with the *Kriyas* of Kapalabhati we fire-fan abdominal energy. Now we develop and strengthen the abdomen further and deeper by churning the whole pelvic-abdominal area into one unified space and then link it in Bhastrika with the thoracic space of the chest. The three sections of the trunk *pelvis, abdomen & thorax* are themselves technically threefold divided:

Vajroli, Mula and Aswini for the pelvis.

Naulis, Kapalabhatis and Uddhiyana for the abdomen.

Uddhiyana, Bhastrika and Ujjaya for the thorax.

The *pelvis* is externally opened and stabilized by hip-opening *Asana* and internally contacted primarily with *Mula-bandha* and the help of *Vajroli & Aswini.*

To point out the connecting and central role of the abdomen, we further dissect it into the *pelvic-, central- & thoracic-abdomen.* Anatomically their dissections are resembled by the three horizontal ›tendious intersections‹ running across the abdomen (and make together with the ›linea Alba‹ for the ›washboard-like-design‹ in a fitness-trained body).

The *pelvic-abdomen* shows its internal strength in the controlled ability of ›letting-go‹ or ›popping out‹ the *inguinal ligaments* through *Nauli2*. The **central-abdomen,** strengthened and vitalised through the Kriya of *Kapalabhatis,* becomes tuned and toned through *Nabhi-bandha* and the Kriya of *Nauli1*. The **thoracic-abdomen** is touched by *Uddhiyana-bandha.*

The *thorax* develops, strengthens and extends through stable *Uddhiyana,* dynamic *Bhastrika* and still *Ujjaya.*

In *Nauli1* it is the *recti abdomini* (abdominals) which are ›popped out‹; while in *Nauli2* it is the *inguinal ligaments* which are ›popped out‹. While *Nauli2* is performed static and held on either or both sides, *Nauli1* can be done on one or both sides and also dynamically by churning it in wave-like motions in either direction.

The *Naulis* might take a while before coming out nicely and it is primarily a practice of establishing Uddhiyana-bandha, which works, strengthens and lengthens the right regions within and creates the necessary space and surface. The ›letting go‹ of the Naulis is a symptomatic effect of a well done Uddhiyana-bandha. *Uddhiyana as the abhyasic effort and Nauli as the vairagyic letting go.*

Bhastrika Kriya
... flaring Agni shakti up & awakening the Prana shakti ...

While the agnisaric Kriyas of *Kapalabhati* are the ›fanning‹ of Agni-shakti, the agnisaric Kriya of *Bhastrika* is the ›flaring up‹ of Agni-shakti high into the spacious chest of Prana-shakti.
The pelvis roots us with Mula-bandha and the central-abdominal area centres us with Nabhi-bandha. With Uddhiyana-bandha we shift up touching thoracic space. This touch of the abdominal-thoracic space becomes established through *Bhastrika* and connects the vertical space needed for Ujjaya.

In *Bhastrika* it is Nabhi-bandha which keeps us alert, supported by ongoing Mula-bandha. The strong vertical respiration flares high into the chest where it awakens the spacious essence of *Prana-shakti* and setting free the pranayamic expansion of the breath.
Here the spacious stability of the body within Asana and the dynamic of the breath are essential. It is the breath which moves the (visceral) body within its physical structure; otherwise having lost the effortless stability of Asana it would be a pushing & pulling of the breath by the shoulders.
From the waist down we are firmly rooted in Asana triggered by Mula-bandha and from the waist up we are moved by the action of vertical fire-breath performing *Bhastrika-kriya.*

Ujjaya
... from locking the Mula to sealing the Jalandhara via Ujjaya ...

Ujjaya (victorious or uprising) is the established connected vertical breath. It is the mode of breathing which, if refined, makes for the natural pranayamic rhythm, its variations and modulations. Staying emphatically with the respirational aspect of *Ujjaya,* it will turn us inward, sense-absorbed and shifting into Pratyahara. *The ultimate motive of Ujjaya or pranayamic breathing is to minimise the movement of the breath and to maximise its duration; to make it long (dirgha) and subtle (sukshma) as defined in Y.S.2.50.*

The possible sound of *Ujjaya* is to slow down and lengthen the breath. It is done by slightly contracting the space inside the throat (between the vocal cords) sounding like ›a gentle resonant snore‹. *Ujjaya* is the turning inward from nasal into throat breathing or *from oxygenetic respiration into pranic inspiration.* Technically it is the cartilaginous action of the glottis, which is felt as a contractive sensation within the larynx. It can vary from a quite audible motion ›aspirating through the bottleneck of the glottis‹, to a quiet and inaudible notion of fine elongated breath passing almost unnoticed through our respirational tract. The audible motion might be used as an ongoing *jappa* or recitation of ›so‹ with the inhale and ›ham‹ with the exhale meaning ›He-I am‹. The inaudible notion of *Ujjaya* might be used as ongoing *a-jappa* or soundless internalisation of the former meaning.

Our sense of direction is bodily derived from the vertical spinal structure holding us upright, and respirationally from the voluminous action of the vertical three-lobed lungs. *Ujjaya* is the connective and lungfulfilling breath travelling inside our bandhic space and expands into the realm of Pranayama ... the art of inhale, exhale and transition.

With Mula-bandha we hook the breath on to the spine, fasten it with Nabhi-bandha and ride it along the spine-line high into the chest, spaciously expanding in every direction and eventually binding it ›in the final touch within the throat‹, the sealing action of Jalandhara-bandha – that is the inspiration of Ujjaya.

Jalandhara Bandha
... the closing of the snare & sealing the kumbha ...

Jalandhara-bandha or the ›*snare that closes the upper net*‹ seals the upper trunk and makes it ready for Pranayama to take place. It unfolds at the apex of inhalation through the inflating thoracic diaphragm into the base of the neck. With the complete filling of the lungs the apes or upper ends rise higher than the thoracic borderline of the clavicles and push up into the neck. This touch-sensation is felt as *Jalandhara-bandha.*

The jalandharic area is the borderline between upper chest and neck. Its action within the throat is marked by the clavicles and sternum, their joint and notch in the front; the cervical spine at the back and the ›atlas‹ at the top (first cervical vertebrae with a for-backward sliding ability). *Note that this cone shaped jalandharic cavity has a longer back (nape) and a shorter front (throat).* The triggering sensation of the inflating lungs into the throat is *Jalandhara-bandha.* This means that the vertical motion of Ujayya extends the nape up through cervical elongation, which rises the back of the head, pushes the atlas slightly forward and initiates the downward move of the chin, thus meeting the upcoming notch (sternum) halfway.

The art of Jalandhara-bandha is to allow thoracic space to extend into the base of the neck, initiating the up-move of the nape and down-move of the chin. This seals the gross respiration, preventing an uncontrolled pranic blow into the head and channels its finer entities into the brain, crown of the head and *brahmarandhra*. »The word jala refers to the brain and the nerve passing through the neck. Dhara denotes the upward pull.«
-Sw. Vishnudevananda p.247-

The common translation of *Jalandhara-bandha* as ›chin-lock‹ or pressing the chin down is therefore only a symptomatic expression of an integral internal process. Rather than dropping the chin we want to understand the *spatial-gravitational* mechanics happening within our bodily framework. A drooping chin might still allow a great deal of gross respirational energy to shoot up into the head, making it dizzy and unstable. A well performed *Jalandhara-bandha* on the other hand seals the trunk and makes us enjoy the pranic dance within with a pleasantly buzzed (the joy of sukha) but clear and centred head.

... conclusion & transition ...

We lift the pelvic floor and trigger the spinal process with MULA-BANDHA, which shifts the momentum up into the abdomen where we hold it with NABHI-BANDHA. We cultivate and establish the pelvic-abdominal area through the KRIYAS of KAPALABHATI and NAULI-KRIYAS. We counter gravity and shift the momentum further up into the thoracic space with UDDHIYANA-BANDHA and the KRIYA of BHASTRIKA. It is the vertical breath of UJJAYA that unifies all those spaces in its journey upwards and seals the trunk in its upper opening through JALANDHARA-BANDHA.

With the practice of **Mudra** we develop sensitivity and amplify internal tendencies until we can understand, differentiate and reintegrate them into a bigger picture ... *the yogic principle of inner understanding instead of outer control.*

>>It was not that he (Goraksha) believed that the practice of bodily contortions or control of bodily functions was the final of Yoga, nor was he under the delusion that such control of the body would, in and by itself, produce Samadhi and self-realisation. What he did and quite rightly, was to emphasise the irrevocable necessity of going through the lower stages, which are apt to neglected and ignored because they seem so difficult, and by a process of wishful thinking unnecessary.<<
- A.K. Banerjea 1962; also cited in M. Burely 2000

PRACTICE

Uddhiyana Bandha and the Kriyas of Nauli 1&2

Uddhiyana-bandha in Uddhiyanabandhasana:

… stand with your feet mat-width apart, feet parallel and hands on the hip-bones.

… exhale the navel back and then 15-20 breaths in Kapalabhati 1.

… after last exhalation pause with firm Nabhi-bandha and then inhale vertically and spaciously into an open throat, looking up.

… bend the legs and thrust the trunk for and down with a full exhale through the mouth; keep the lower back extended.

… finish complete exhale, put your palms on the middle or upper thighs (with the fingers pointing in), pull the navel back as in a vacuum and come up with bend legs into straight arms, sucking the abdominal contents as high as possible into the diaphragm inducing Jalandhara bandha; hold and stay in *bhaya Kumbhaka.*

… before coming out tie the navel further back (giving a little expiration-al jerk), bend the legs more, extend the lower back and come up with a vertical inhalation into standing, touching Jalandhara-bandha and remain in *antara Kumbhaka.*

… exhale, relax in the breath and repeat.

… after the last time lift the arms up in front and above the head to stretch and release the abdomen; after a while exhale into easy forward-hanging Uttanasana.

Nauli 1 in Uddhiyanabandhasana:

... perform Uddhiyana-bandha as described and pop out Nauli 1 by relaxing the *recti abdomini* forward with the rest of the abdomen holding back; push the arms into the thighs and slightly round the lower back. Play with the details to make Nauli happen.

... Nauli 1 to the right is done by letting go the right *rectus abdominus*; Nauli 1 to the left is done by letting go the left *rectus abdominus*; while the central Nauli 1 is done by letting go both *recti abdomini*.

... once this is established start to churn the centre Nauli in wave-like motions from left to right 5 to 25 times; change sides (from right to left) in the next round.

... before coming out shortly return to central Nauli and Uddhiyana-bandha and come up as described.

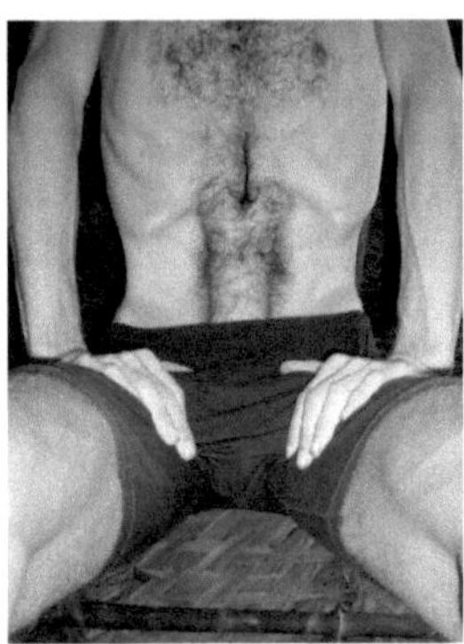

Nauli 2 in Uddhiyanabandhasana:

... perform Uddhiyana-bandha, hold it and bring space and awareness as far down the abdomen as possible.

... pop out Nauli 2 by ›releasing‹ the *inguinal ligaments;* first alternate sides and then together; play with the details to make it happen.

... before coming out return shortly to Nauli 1 and Uddhiyana and then up as described.

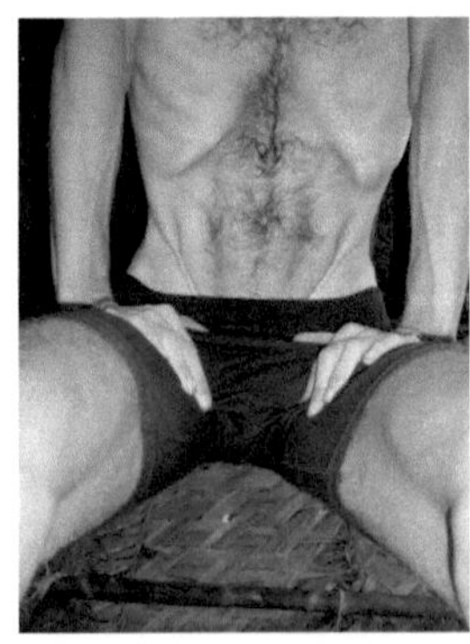

Agnisari-Kriyas of Kapalabhati

Kapalabhati 1:

... sit in (Vira-)Asana, exhale and pull the navel back towards the spine.

... in- & exhale strongly by pushing the belly out with the inhale and pulling it back in with the exhale in a pumping motion.

... do this about 30-50 times, then finish with an exhalation and stay in *bhaya Kumbaka*, holding Nabhi- and Mula-bandha.

... inhale vertically and remain in *antara Kumbhaka* with Nabhi and Mula.

... gradually and with firm Nabhi-bandha exhale slow and even all the way down touching Mula-bandha.

... relax in the breath and repeat.

Kapalabhati 2:

... sit in (Vira-)Asana, first exhale and then inhale the navel out.

... strongly & firmly exhale the belly back for 40-60 times, letting the inhales occur and ›recoil‹ by themselves.

... after the last exhale stay in *bhaya Kumbhaka* with firm Nabhi- and Mula-bandha.

... keeping the Nabhi inhale vertically and remain in *antara Kumbhaka.*

... with firm Nabhi exhale gradually, slow and even vertically down along the spine, until touching Mula-bandha.

... relax in the breath and repeat.

Kapalabhati 3:

... sit in (Vira-)Asana, exhale and inhale the navel out.

... firm & strongly exhale the navel back to its maximum.

... remain in *bhaya Kumbhaka* and continuously sucking the navel back.

or

... remain in *bhaya Kumbhaka* and strongly pump the belly out and in for as many times as it goes (as in mock abdominal breathing).

or

... remain in *bhaya Kumbhaka* and strongly move in vertical motions up and down along the spine-line for as many times as it goes (as in mock vertical breathing).

… finish by pulling the navel a bit further back (with a slight expirational jerk) and then slow & steady inhale vertical high into the chest, remaining in *antara Kumbhaka* with Nabhi- and Mula-Bandha.

… increase Nabhi-bandha and exhale slow & even all the way down to the Mula and remain in *bhaya Kumbhaka*.

… repeat or rest in the breath.

Agnisari – Kriya of Bhastrika

… sit in (Padma-)Asana, exhale the navel back and push the sitting bones.

… strong, deep but not speedy in & exhale 10-30 times vertically from the abdomen high into the chest and down again (between navel & heart); keeping Mula-bandha either throughout or at least in the inhales (suck it up with the inhale and squeeze it down with the exhale).

… after the last exhale pull the navel firmly back and remain in *bhaya Kumbhaka* with Nabhi and Mula.

… with firm Nabhi inhale vertically touching Jalandhara and remain in *antara Kumbhaka* with the Bandhas.

… keeping Nabhi-bandha exhale slowly and even; rebalance and relax in the breath and repeat.

Ujjaya – the pranayamic breath

... sit in (Siddha-)Asana and exhale the navel back.
... inhale slow, even & steady vertically from the Mula via the Nabhi all the way up along the spine-line (with lengthening waist, opening ribcage and widening chest) until touching and sealing the inner throat with Jalandhara-bandha.
... remain in *antara Kumbhaka* with Mula, Nabhi and Jalandhara.
... exhale gradually and even more slow with Nabhi-bandha down to the Mula and remain in *bhaya Kumbhaka* with the Bandhas.
... repeat or rest in the breath.

Jalandhara Bandha

... sit in (Siddha-)Asana and exhale the navel back.
... inhale vertically and completely.
... channel the vertical breath through the chest into the breastbone and sterno-clavicular notch, where the upper lobes of the lung extend and touch into the base of the neck, inducing Jalandhara-bandha and meeting with the down-coming chin (because of respirational nape extension).
... remain in *antara Kumbhaka* with the Bandhas.
... exhale vertically long and gradual, softening Jalandhara.
... remain in *bhaya Kumbhaka* with the Bandhas (including a slight Jalandhara).
... repeat or rest in the breath.

PRANAYAMA
Puraka, Kumbhaka & Rechaka ... in Asana

Puraka   Stability

Kumbhaka   Dynamic

Rechaka   Stillness

**The inhale teaches the exhale and both reveal the transition ...
Kumbhaka takes over. The stability of Puraka holds the dynamic of Kumbhaka
and releases into the stillness of Rechaka.**

»Prana means the vitality of life which expresses itself through the various centres of
the body. Its simple meaning is energy. Pranayama means the regulation of the
control of prana (vital energy) in three stages: inhalation, retention and exhalation of
breath ... Even normal respiration has three stages which go on all the time,
wether we practice Pranayama or not. These are breathing in, breathing
out and holding the breath for a while with ease. All types of Pranayama consist of
particular combination of these three processes.«
- Sw. Satyananda; ›Dynamics of Yoga‹, B.S.Y. p.42&44 -

Intro

Starting to understand the respirational process happens during the pratice of Asana and Mudra resulting in the established vertical breath of *Ujjaya*. In *Pranayama* we use this mode of breathing as the base for further subtlefication, its modifications and variations. Lengthening and rhythmifying the breath, we experience *inhalation – transition – exhalation – transition* as the interactive phases of the breath with its *respirational & transitional* (respirational-less) tendencies continuously triggering and bringing each other forth.

Inhaling and exhaling we breathe air containing various quantities of gaseous and pranic qualities. The normal emphasis in breathing is on the oxygenation of the bloodstream to meet the demand for metabolic sustenance with only little space left for pranic vitalisation. In Pranayama we need less gaseous respiration (oxygenation) and are more receptive for its pranic unfoldment. Ultimately we need very little oxygenation to maintain ourselves and have potentially a huge capacity for pranic vitalisation. *The sincere practice of Pranayama transforms the breath moving gaseous air containing vital prana, into more vital prana and less gaseous air.*

On a mundane level the art of respiration is being essential, where the vitality for metabolic sustenance happens continuously on a celluar life-maintaining level.
On a pranayamic level the art of transition is being essential, where the respirational process refines into its own trans-solution and is pranic-ly sustained ... *where the ›Prana-lingam‹ of his breath merges into the ›Pranayoni‹ of her retention.*

Pranayama consists of respiration *(Puraka & Rechaka),* transition *(Kumbhaka)* and transcendence *(Chathurta)* of the breath. Puraka & Rechaka deal with the *respirational,* Kumbhaka with the *transitional* and Chathurta with the *transcendental* quality of the breath.

The inhalation reveals the exhalation which reveals the transition and the transition reveals the transcendence. This wants to be decently understood as we become progressively aware of the pranic action within: that nothing new emerges, is added or subtracted. That we deal with one process (breath) which reveals, through practical refinement its tendencies and patterns. These tendencies are naturally there but normally are to minuscule to be recognised and understood. It is our continuous abhyasic effort that amplifies, refines and understands the same process from its origin to its originality – *the process of the breath. As the essence of Asana is already ingrained in the gross and conditioned body, the essence of Pranayama is already ingrained in the unrefined and contracted breath.*

Puraka provides for the *stability* of steady and smooth inhalation, *Kumbhaka* provides for the *dynamic* of vibrant and smooth transition and *Rechaka* provides for the *stillness* of even and smooth exhalation. On the surface *Puraka & Rechaka* continuously inhale and exhale the experience of respiration, while underneath we discern its pattern and refine it into its own (respiration-less) transition. This process, if sufficiently understood and practised, prolongs into the ›retention‹ of *Kumbhaka.*

It is *Sahita*-Kumbhaka, when it is volitional induced and *Kevala*-Kumbhaka when it occurs spontaneously (as a result of pranayamic integration and not of pathological condition as in apnoea). With *Kevala*-Kumbhaka we have one possible mode for the fourth aspect of Pranayama *Chathurta,* which transcends the common three qualities of the breath.

Within Kumbhaka itself, even so apparently retentive and static, happens the necessary metabolic sustenance, which nourishes and maintains that what needs to be nourished and maintained. To be exposed into the nakedness of retention without respiration to cover up for is highly purifying and transformative.

Part 1

PRANAYAMAS

The various Pranayamas are variations and modulations of our natural pranayamic rhythm *(Sahaja Vritti)*, which develops and refines out of Ujjaya (our established vertical breath). Ujjaya becomes *Sahaja Vritti* when it is lengthened & subtlefied to its maximum, of course still within the context of a stable and rhythmic breath. *To maximise the duration and to minimise the movement of the breath* is the way to do it.

This natural pranayamic rhythm *(Sahaja Vritti)* has two variations and various modifications. It variies by becoming either ›even‹ *(Sama Vritti)* or ›uneven‹ *(Visama Vritti)*. The modifications come by using different emphasizes as in nostril (both or alternate) or oral (Shitali, Sitkari) breathing, with or without sound or using visualization and imagination. Here we concern ourselves with the three main rhythms and two modifications to keep it essential.

SAHAJA-, VISAMA- & SAMA-VRITTI ... the natural, the uneven & the even rhythm:
Being in the pranayamic breath we have three options (or waves) for rhythmic breathing: *Sahaja-vritti* the natural wave, where the breath flows in its natural capacity for respiration and transition. *Visama-vritti* the uneven wave, where the periods for respiration and transition differ; and *Sama-vritti* the even wave, where the periods for respiration and transition are the same.

To keep the respirational ratios in *Visama-* or *Sama-vritti* might seem manageable, while their transitional durations could seem difficult. Practice shows that the capacity for Kumbhaka grows with the refined understanding and capability for Puraka & Rechaka. *This means that by altering the quality of respiration, we also alter the capacity for transition.* The quality of visamic respiration contains the capacity for visamic transition and the same goes for samic respiration and transition.

To prevent prejudice over ›even and uneven‹ it is good to remember that our natural breath normally flows visama-vrittic or uneven with the exhalation being longer than the inhalation. While the even balance of Sama-vritti is often our volitional effort for pranic equalisation.

Sahaja-vritti is the longest-finest *(dirgha-sukshma Y.S.2.50)* possible flow of the breath according to pranayamic capacity; following its own natural ratio still, stable and rhythmic.

The given ratio for *Visama-vritti* is 1:4:2:1, pertaining to the durations of inhalation-transition-exhalation-transition. A practical approach here could be to start with $1:2:2:\frac{1}{2}$ and gradually breathing into 1:3:2:1 and 1:4:2:1.

The given ratio for *Sama-vritti* is 2:2:2:2; a realistic approach towards Sama-vritti could be to start with $2:1:2:\frac{1}{2}$ and gradually breathing into 2:2:2:1 and 2:2:2:2.

The actual amount of time and practice needed to approximate Vi-Sama-vrittis depends upon our personal capacity and fitness for pranayamic receptivity. *The quality of our practice depends upon the effort we put into understanding the tendencies of respiration and letting the retention develop itself out of the transitional process ... rather than trying to maintain a static hold over it.*

ANULOMA & VILOMA ... with or against the hair-flow:

Loma or the *hair-flow* indicates the directive flow of the breath. Going Anuloma or *with the hair* means to flow with the natural tendency of the breath, while going Viloma or *against the hair,* means our volitional effort to break and interrupt the natural tendency of the breath. Attentively done they are most efficient to strengthen and lengthen the breath. The volitional effort to alter the cycle of the breath with *Viloma* (interrupting the natural breath-flow) touches repeatedly the transitional dynamic of the breath and makes it thus increasingly understood. The flow of *Anuloma* follows the natural tendency of the breath to inhale deeply, filling the lungs to capacity with a little prolonged transition; while the exhale is slow and gradual, completely emptying the lungs and remaining shortly in empty transition.

Our *Anuloma* breath is defined by a deep and full inhalation, its spacious transition, followed by an even and long exhalation and a recollectional transition in empty beingness. Anuloma can be very akin to Sahaja-vritti but differs as it follows set ratios, while in Sahaja we follow our natural rhythm.
Viloma breaks the flow into several stages to consciously intersect the breath, for understanding its tendencies and strengthening its capacity, i.e.: inhale-stop; inhale-stop; inhale-stop; exhale-stop; exhale-stop; exhale-stop.

NADISHODHANA ... & the three currents:

Nadishodhana is the quality of the breath used for purification *(shodhana)* of the pranic currents or *Nadis* which we have so plentifull within us; according to yogic cosmology between 72 – 350000. Apparently this vast network of *Nadis* boils down to three major currents, with two running along either side of the spine, criss-crossing (or running parallel) several plexi or chakras along their route and one running within the spine itself. These three main currents are termed *Ida Nadi* (moon, yamuna, left nostril), *Pingala Nadi* (sun, ganga, right nostril) and *Shushumna Nadi* (saraswati, both nostrils or none).

It is significant that according to Hatha-Yoga, these Nadis are accessible respirationally via the nostrils and that the harmonisation of *Ida & Pingala Nadi* through alternate nostril-breathing results in pranic balance and the *kundalinic* flow within *Shushumna*. This also symbolizes another possible mode of the fourth pranayamic aspect *Chathurta,* where the three modes of breathing are transcended and absorbed within *shushumnic* unity.

This process of harmonisation between *Ida & Pingala Nadi* symbolises in an archaic way the hatha-yogic effort to harmonise and balance the dual principles within us, represented by *ha* (sun) & *tha* (moon), and merging them into *advaitic* unity.

And even so there is an obvious ›geographical‹ resemblance between the *nadis & chakras* in yogic cosmology and the cerebral system of para-sympathetic *nerves & plexi* in medical science, there is no actual need to hypothetically equate them. In case such desires arise we better check whether the incentive and motivation behind is still coming from our curiosity for yogic inquiry or from the urge of our speculative mind.

The calming and balancing effect of *Nadishodhana* upon our nervous and pranic system is easily experienced if practiced and we do need this ›calm-balm‹ to be less mental and more pranic aware for further yogic proceedings. In all Pranayamas we want to assimilate this balancing, harmonizing and purifying quality of *Nadishodhana;* and in the specific practice of *Nadishodhana* itself we use alternate nostril breathing as a means to access this harmonization. Such alternation accesses and balances *Ida & Pingala Nadi* directly and efficiently. Most Pranayamas can be done with both or alternate nostrils and even the Kriyas of Agnisari can be done so. *The thus balanced and purified breath moves in sahajic-visamic-samic rhythms or in anulomic-vilomic modulations and electrifies the Nadis into beaming and vibrant pranic currents, sparking up our system and vitality.*

Part 2

KUMBHAKA

In most yogic scriptures pertaining to the technical performance of Pranayama, much and little has been said about the nature of *Kumbhaka.* A lot of serpentine and divine properties are attributed to it and it is well expounded in the abstract sense of symbology while little has been said in the concrete sense of detailed instructions. Such symbology can be inspiring, with the almost magical descriptions serving as powerful incentives to ignite our enthusiasm. But such symbology can also be confusing, misleading to fancy expectations for infinite retentions and other wondrous phenomena with all their picturesque powers. And thus missing the point of *Kumbhka* as a self-revealing and unfolding ingridient of the breath.

Some traditions go as far as describing all following limbs from Pratyahara to Samadhi to the prolongation of *Kumbhaka,* as does Sw. Brahmananda in his Jyotsna commentary on H.Y.P.2.12: »When the prana is restrained for a period of one hundred and twenty five palas, then it goes into the brahmarandra. When the prana stays in the brahmarandra for about twenty five palas that is Pratyahara. If it remains there five ghatikas or two hours, it is Dharana. If it stays for sixty ghatikas or one day, it is Dhyana. If it is restrained for twelve days it is Samadhi.«

To equate the prolongation of *Kumbhaka* with *Samadhi* is basically to point out the dormant infinite potential slumbering within our pranic-personal range. But it also illustrates the futillity of expectation, for as long as we are caught up in retentional time, we are also caught up in the endless cycle of prolonging, achieving and becoming. This would ultimately lead to the merged, but still identified state of *prakriti-layanam* (Y.S.1.19) – *instead of breaking out and spiralling this circle into the vertical dimension of vivekic insight, understanding and awakening.*

By truly practising the *Abhyasa* of Pranayama the quality of retention gives us a grasp for the infinite pranic potential within us and *Vairagya* detaches us from egoic temptations to rove in our accomplishment. The effort of retention is checked by the calm and detached flow of the breath in between. We want to stay receptive for that moment (out of time) where the refinement of body & breath subtlefies and merges into mental stillness. Thus accessing personal understanding, we ›crack‹ the pranayamic code without getting lost in it.

The essence of Pranayama is either a respirational harmonisation or a retentive concentration.
The actual Abhyasa of respiration can be a factual practice of Pratyahara.
The actual Abhyasa of retention can be a factual practice of Dharana.

...the dynamic of Kumbhaka...

Within Kumbhaka there is a continuous dynamic keeping the retention linked to the subtle tendency of refined breathing, in which the respiration still flows but respirational-less. The retention is thus a dynamic action where the respirational flow has subsided into its own transition, while the rspirational dynamic still continues and provides for the ease of holding itself. The *bandha-ic* action in Kumbhaka adapts to the changing space conditions of the lungs and creates a spatial support and comfort for the various volumes involved. The possible local strain of holding the breath is a sign that we don't stick to this dynamic and slip (back) into a static and stagnate hold to prolong mechanical time and retentive power.

A certain retentive stamina and capacity is needed no doubt but develops itself mainly symptomatic in our practice with no need to get lost in temporal expectations. An effective approach to directly enhance our retentive capacity is to combine *Kumbhaka* with *Bhastrikas,* holding the breath with empty as well with full lungs.

Actually we don't hold the breath in Kumbhaka but refine the respiration into its own transition or dissolution and it is this aspect which secures the thoracic volume in each stage. Otherwise strain might set in when the volume-space of the lungs either extend or shrink within their comfort zone and in both cases loosing their internal base – the ground beneath ones feet. This *comfort zone* is very well explained in the second chapter of »Science of breath« (Himalayan press; Honesdale, Pennsylvania 1979) written by Alan Hymes regarding the mechanism of the breath; especially his explanation of the alveoli and their surface tension in connection with diaphragmic action during the breath. It is this surface tension which enables an always relaxed diaphragm even when it is compressed or stretched.

Therefore at the stage of practicing prolonged pranayamic rhythms, the physical (asanic & mudric) aspect of the body should be firm and spacious enough to accommodate and adapt to the various stages of the retentional process. The limit of our retentional capacity should be triggered by the need for respirational expression and not physical discomfort.

Gradually in the course of Pranayama any respirational or retentional discomfort wants to be overcome by the asanic conditions of ›sthira, sukha & ananta-samapatti‹ pertaining to the body of breath.

Part 3

Prana & Space

To better understand *Pranayama,* its ›ayama‹ (expansion) and ›yama‹ (control), we need to go deeply into its energetic essence, into the nature of Space & Prana: conscious space (body) and pranic awareness (breath), where the *ayama* of *Prana* expands the breath into its own dissolution and *yama*-ic restrain. As the physical body refines itself into structural space through Asana & Mudra, the vital breath in Pranayama refines itself into pranic space … *and the pranic space bridges the still mind into transmental silence.*

… a pranic mystery or the story of space …

Space or *akasha* is the most refined and transformative element *Prakriti* has to offer and is the borderline up to which our personal inquiry can take ourselves – *space is the place!* Prana (breath) is the essence of Space (body) and also born out of it, they enable us to witness and experience (mind).

Om Purnamada Purnamidam
Purnat Purnamudachyate
Purnasya Purnamadaya
Purnamevavashishyate

Space always is … neither full nor empty … always complete.
Empty space out of space … the full emptiness of space remains.

Wherever space is created, prana comes into being.
Where space opens, prana is; where prana is, space opens.
Where there is pranic awareness, there is conscious space.
Where prana is, self-awareness can take place through space.
Where space is, consciousness can be witnessed through prana.
Prana in space is life in mystery.

To re-establish Space & Prana into their original mystery we need to blow our breath & mind into the vital place of non-conceptual but perceptual dynamics and unfoldings … *into space the vital place of life.* Therefore in Pranayama we inquire deeply into that dynamic which weaves the energetic pattern of our being into the web of life: *sensation-respiration-fluctuation or thinking-feeling-acting.*

… from breath-breathing-breather to breath-breathing-being breathed …

Due to repetitive ignorance and illusion we lost our birthright of a natural firm body, a natural flowing breath and a natural tranquil mind. The practice of Yoga is therefore to re-establish us into the personal qualities of stability, mobility & tranquillity. Such a practice in its own ashtangic time and *kriya-ic* unfoldment may lead to a elemental experience of space within mental stillness – the density of reality – and may even slip into the transpersonal perception of silence or *shunya* the trans-elemental (and therefore also trans-spatial) void. *From the stability of the body, the dynamic of the breath & the stillness of the mind into the transmental silence of space-lessness.*

Through structural and respirational elongation and expansion we rediscover Space and promote Prana. The embodied pranic space of breath & mind expresses itself through the personal vehicle of the body. Pranic space is mental stillness. *The pranic space of the breath respirates our body into being and the pranic matter of the mind thinks our body into being.*

In the great expanse of existence or *maha-akash, Prana* the vital principle and *Chitta* the conscious principle embody themselves as *breath & mind,* with the elemental body to contain them. The air of the breath and the thought of the mind dissolve in Prana & Chitta. Ultimately and absolutely we merge as *Prana-shakti* (Shakti) into the witnessing consciousness of *Chit-shakti* (Shiva). Now in this spacious context we once again see the futility to attempt a duality between body & mind, which are essentially made up from the same stuff – pranic matter individually manifested in space. *Because of Prana there is* **space** *(of which)* **matter & energy** *(are its expressions).*

... the threefold unity of gunatic qualities ...

The natural condition of life is to change. The nature of this change provides for the energy of life. This energy has three interdependent qualities, mingling and singling our experiences into the one vital expression, which we call our life. These qualities, properties or characters are called *gunas* and also *shilas* (Y.S.2.18/19). They provide for our need to express life individually and also to let life express itself universally.

<pre>
Sthiti   – tamas – stability – actuality   – matter – stability
Kriya   – rajas – dynamic – activity   – energy – mobility
Prakasha – satvas – stillness – potentiality – space – tranquillity
</pre>

Ultimately they unify back into their destiny – the source of the Self.
They express and manifest themselves individually through:

<pre>
matter of body   – **stability** – structural space
energy of breath – **dynamic** – vital space
space of mind   – **stillness** – elemental space
</pre>

Matter *(kaya),* energy *(prana)* & space *(mana)* are the expressions of individualised Life and have the cosmic qualities of stability, dynamic & stillness, which are personalised as body, breath & mind. All of them share the same common essence or conscious energy *(Shiva as Prana-Shakti). Prana is (in) individual Life and individual Life is (through) Prana.*

»From the Self is born Prana. Just as there is a shadow when a body is there, so Prana is fixed on the Self. It comes to this body owing to the actions of the mind.«
(Prashna Upanishad 3.3)

Yoga makes the abhyasic effort to express the unexpressible nature of that what is – the nature of Prana: non-conceptual but perceptual – not mental but experimental – for the practical sake of experiencing it, and not for the theoretical sake of mentalising about it. *The mind-blowing nature of Prana, the essence of all life, vibrates our person into Being.*

Thus we experience *Prana* throughout the layers *(shariras & koshas)* of our being. As the self-generating dynamic in shifting qualities *(gunas)* and as unfolding conductors and wondrous phenomena *(nadis, chakras, granthis)* arising within the cosmic framework of our individual boundaries.

COSMOGONY OF PRANA

»The seat of the *prana* is the heart; of the *apana* the anus; of the *samana* the region around the navel; of the *udana* the throat; while the *vyana* moves throughout the body.«
- ›Shiva Samhita‹ 3.7 -

Prana
... & the five prana-Vayus ...

direction	vayu	seat	function
up	prana	heart	respiration
down	apana	anus	excretion
centering	samana	navel	digestion
down	udana	throat	deglution (swallow)
circulating	vyana	all-pervading	circulation

... the combustion of prana & apana ...

»Prana and apana are the twin aspects of Mahaprana. The direction of motion of apana is downward and prana is upward. They move in an opposite direction in order to balance the Prana throughout the body.«
(›Early teachings of Sw. Satyananda Saraswati‹, B.S.Y. 1988)

Now in bandhic applied Pranayama the two main **Vayus,** prana & apana become reversed in their directive flow. **Apana**-Vayu gets reversed through *Mula-bandha* and supported in its new upward direction through *Nabhi-bandha* or *Uddhiyana*. **Prana**-Vayu gets reversed through *Jalandhara-bandha* and supported in its new downward direction trough **udana**-Vayu. They meet, combust and fuse within **samana**-Vayu in the abdominal region; from here they spread and circulate throughout the body via **vyana**-Vayu.

Mula-bandha moves the muddy waters of *apana-Vayu* and its psychic deposits from our pelvic-samskaric pool up into the abdominal bowl, so that they can get released and evaporated in the clarifying even-ness of *samana-Vayu*. The damp quality of *apana-Vayu* threatens to weaken the digestive power of Agni-shakti and her potential to transform food into nutrition, emotions into equanimity and instinctive fears into inspirational intuitions. Therefore with Jalandhara-bandha we blow the pure air of *prana-Vayu* down, kindling and fanning the gastric fire of Agni-shakti and burning the dampness of rising *apana-Vayu*.

Mula-shakti stirs our impurities up through reversed apana-Vayu and Mula-bandha.
Prana-shakti blows her purity down through reversed prana-Vayu and Jalandhara-bandha.
Agni-shakti burns and transforms in the centeredness of samana-Vayu and Nabhi-bandha.

APANA	SAMANA	PRANA
Water-------------------------->>>*Fire*<<<----------------------------------*Air*		
[--------------------------->>>----**combustio**n----<<<----------------------]		
Mula	Nabhi/Uddhiyana	Jalandhara
Mula-Shakti	**Agni-Shakti**	**Prana-Shakti**

A minute pranic combustion for vital maintainance or metabolic susteinance takes place continiously at the level of the cells through the gaseous exchange in the bloodstream, depending on the quality of the breathing lungs and pumping heart. The more vibrant the breath and heart, the more efficient is this biochemical exchange during its vene-ous and artery-ous course. The pranayamic combustion of apana & prana within samana is a highly refined and potently amplified version of this metabolic process. Through the volitional act of Bandha and Kumbhaka in Asana, we mutate this metabolic-cellular process into a pranic-atomic fusion, blowing the essence of Prana into action, which purifies burns and frees us from deep-seated conditionings. This pranic combustion is the ignition which sparks up the slumber of our vital essence – *Prana-shakti.*

... a little note on udana, samana & vyana ...

Udana, moving between head and navel, has the opposite flow of prana and is thus very suited to support prana in its reversion. It regulates the swallowing act of deglutition and coordinates our voice and sound ability which roughly symbolises the openess of Vishuddhi-chakra, our throat centre. Jalandhara-bandha reverses prana and also reinforces udana in its direction from the larynx down. As the action of Mula-bandha reversing apana is safely embedded within the pelvic structure (and also has Nabhi-bandha as support), the action of Jalandhara-bandha reversing prana needs the additional help of udana to secure and maintain stability in the subtleness of the neck.

Samana is the equalising Vayu centring around the navel and providing for the digestive combustion of apana & prana, in which matter transforms into energy and into the pranic harmony of a even functioning biological rhythm.

Vyana circulates this harmonious biological rhythm from the navel throughout the body, distributing and integrating the several functions into one living experience.

... conclusion & transition ...

While the established vertical breath of Ujjaya unfolds through the external and internal alignment of the body and its space, it is in the prolonged & refined rhythmic balance of the breath (its respiration & transition), where the potential of *Pranayama* lies; embodied by *Asana* and supported by *Mudra.*

»Pranayama occupies the most important position in Hatha-Yoga. It essentially consists in the conquest of the whole biological system in man, the awakenment and concentration of vital power and the upward movement of the unwasted and concentrated vital energy in the direction of union with the Supreme Spirit. The well-planned and well-pursued regulation and control of the breath is the key to this adventure ... The breathing apparatus is related to all the inner organs of the body.«
- ›An introduction to Natha-Yoga‹; Goraknath mandir, Gorakhpur -

PRACTICE

Vishnu-mudra & Nadishodhana

Vishnu-mudra is performed by tucking in the index & middle finger of either hand (traditionally the right), while keeping ring & little finger straight out to one side and the thumb to the other. Keep the hand in front of the nose with a slight touch of the ring & little finger on one and the thumb on the other nostril, which can then be closed by increasing the finger pressure accordingly for alternate nostril breathing.
Important is the arm position with the elbow pointing out enough to the side to avoid contraction on that side of the chest; it should not become tiring or distractive. It is helpful to imagine a raw egg under the armpit, which neither wants to be cracked nor to fall down.

... sit in Asana and apply Vishnu-mudra, blocking the right nostril and exhaling through the left.
... inhale through the left, close and remain in antara Kumbhaka.
... open the right nostril, exhale and remain in bhaya Kumbhaka.
... inhale through the right, close and remain in antara Kumbhaka.
... open the left nostril, exhale and remain in bhaya Kumbhaka.
... repeat in rhythm (Sahaja or Vi-Sama) or modification (Anu/Viloma) of choice.
... relax in the breath, repeat or continue.

Bandha-trayam (the threefold lock)

In *Bandha-tryam* (which is also one form of *Maha-bandha* or the ›great binding‹) we apply the three main Bandhas, which seal our pelvic, abdominal and thoracic cavities during Kumbhaka. We have already experienced *Bandha-tryam* in standing *Uddhiyana-bandhasana*. The classic pose for Bandha-tryam is Padmasana for stability reasons; otherwise we approximate it in a stable fashion.
In every Pranayama the quality of Puraka & Rechaka determine the retentive capacity for Kumbhaka. Every full cycle of Pranayama has its climax internally in the *Bandha-tryam* of *antara Kumbhaka,* which is done (unless we are really quite advanced) with Nabhi-bandha; externally it has its climax in *bhaya Kumbhaka,* either deeply with Uddhiyana or steadily with Nabhi-bandha; Mula and Jalandhara (as ongoing as possible) are the other two Bandhas.
It is especially here in *Bandha-tryam,* that the combustive activity (the union of prana & apana within samana) becomes radiant due to the bandhic empowerment of our pranic potential. To imbibe the technique of *Bandha-tryam* we practice it independently and gradually becoming proficient in it, we take it over into the retentions of our pranayamic cycles. As a own practice we start with Agnisaris to charge us up and to develop internal strength needed for our retentive capacity; then applying and reinforcing the Bandhas, we engage actively in both *Kumbhakas* with *Bandha-tryam.*

... sit in (Padm-)Asana exhale the navel back and do 20-40 rounds of any Agnisari.
... with the last exhalation pull the navel strongly back, engage in Uddhiyana and apply Mula and Jalandhara-bandha; remain in bhaya Kumbhaka.
... release Uddhiyana, pull the navel a bit further back and inhale in Ujjaya until the sealing touch of Jalandhara-bandha is felt in the inner throat; remain in antara Kumbhaka with Mula and Nabhi-bandha.
... release slowly and evenly; exhale in Ujjaya until the touch of the Mula.
... relax in the breath and repeat or continue.

Sitting Nauli

The same as in standing *Uddhiyanabandhasana* we practice now in the sitting position (preferably in Padmasana) to further strengthen and reveal the internal abdominal process. A sign of a relatively mastered sitting Nauli is the ability to do *Samanasana*, where we withdraw the hands from the knees and clutching them around the Nauli squeezing and strengthening abdominal *samana*. For spacious reasons, we engage mainly in Nauli1 while sitting ... a little playing is allowed and revealing.

... sit in (Padm-)Asana exhale the navel back and do 20-40 rounds of Kapalabhati 1.
... with the last exhalation draw the navel firmly back, inhale deeply in Ujjaya high into
   the chest, take the chin up and open chest & throat.
... expressively exhale through the mouth, thrusting forward while keeping the knees
   clasped with the hands for stability.
... coming back up, drawing the navel strongly back and up into Uddhiyana-bandha and
   let Nauli 1 pop out.
... remain in static Nauli to either or both sides or churn.
... at the end draw the Nauli back in, fix the navel with a slight expirational pull-back
   and inhale long & full in Ujjaya until the sealing touch in the inner throat.
... remain in antara Kumbhaka.
... exhale slowly and evenly in Ujjaya and remain in bhaya Kumbhaka
   with Nabhi-bandha.
... relax in the breath and repeat or continue.

The following is a suggested **Mudra & Pranayama** practice (inspired and based on the teachings of Clive Sheridan). It unfolds by awakening the various centres through *Bandhas & Kriyas* and then harmonising and balancing *Ujjaya* with *Anu/Viloma & Nadishodhana*. The thus harmonized and balanced breath refines then into the slow rhythms of *Sahaja & Vi-Sama Vrittis*.
There is a fair variety of possible constellations, giving us freedom of choice (and time) to modify and suit our personal practice according to feel and need. The first numbers are given to experiment with and learn the technique. Start with them and once they are established move on to the number in brackets ... always reduce if you feel so.

MUDRA

UDDHIYANABANDHASANA:
... 2x coming up in UDDHIYANA BANDHA.

... 4x coming up in Uddhiyana and popping out NAULI 1; once the Nauli is established
churn it 5 (max.25) times in alternating directions each time.

... 1x coming up in Uddhiyana, popping out NAULI 1 and churn it 5 (max.15) times from
left to right and then 5 (max.15) times from right to left in the same round.

... 1x coming up in Uddhiyana, popping out NAULI 2 and hold – release, pop out NAULI 1
and hold – release, engage in UDDHIYANA and hold – release and come back up
with the inhale.

... relax in the breath and repeat one more time.

After Uddhiyanabandhasana we sit down in Asana.

KAPALABHATI 1:
20x (40) in/out through the left nostril
20x (40) in/out through the right nostril
20x (40) in/out through both nostrils
... repeat 2-3 rounds as described.
... relax in the breath.

KAPALABHATI 2:
40x (80) out through both nostrils
... repeat 2-3 rounds as described.
... relax in the breath

BANDHA TRYAM:
... 3-5 rounds as described.
... release & relax in the breath.

sitting NAULI:
... repeat 1- 3 rounds as described and finish in Samanasana (interlocked hands clasped
around the Nauli, squeezing).
... release & relax in the breath.

BHASTRIKA:
... 10x high into the chest
... repeat 3-5 rounds as described and increase by 5 in each round (10x, 15x, 20x, 25x); put
emphasis on both retentions holding bhaya & antara Kumbhaka for the same length,
increasing time with each round.
... release & relax in the breath.

PRANAYAMA

Having awakened the vital centres with Mudra, we harmonise and balance the breath with the Anu/Viloma flow and Nadishodhana.

VILOMA:
in: 3 stages
hold: 10 (15)
out: 12 (12)
hold: / (5)
... repeat 6-12 rounds as described.
... relax in the breath.

ANULOMA:
in: 7 (10)
hold: 10 (15)
out: 12 (12)
hold: / (5)
... repeat 6-12 rounds as described.
... relax in the breath.

NADISHODHANA:
in: 7 (10)
hold: 10 (15)
out: 12 (12)
hold: / (5)
... repeat 6-12 rounds as described...or in the natural flow of Sahaja Vritti.
... relax in the breath

Having harmonised and balanced the breath, we refine it with the slow rhythms of Sahaja, Visama, & Sama Vritti.

SAHAJA VRITTI:

the longest & finest possible (but still stable and rhythmic) flow of the breath.
... repeat 6-12 rounds.
... relax in the breath.

VISAMAVRITTI:

in: 4 (6)
hold: 16 (24)
out: 8 (12)
hold: 4 (6)
... repeat 6-12 rounds as described.
... relax in the breath.

SAMAVRITTI:

in: 8 (12)
hold: 8 (12)
out: 8 (12)
hold: 8 (12)
... repeat 6-12 rounds as described.
... relax in the breath.

Finish with a few minutes sitting still, releasing and relaxing the breath with no effort whatsoever, being aware of body, space & breath.

SHAVASANA:

For as long as it is needed ... rather longer than shorter.

«The sum and substance of my teaching is this: don't be dishonest to your vital breath; worship that only, abide in that only, accept it as yourself. And when you worship in this manner, it can lead you anywhere, to any heights; this is the quintessence of my talks. Henceforth you are to be identified with the vital breath. Then you will realize, like the sweetness in sugar cane, that this touch of ›I-am-ness‹ which is dwelling in the vital breath, will open up. So understand these words, this advice. Assimilate it and so long as the vital breath is flowing through you, abide in that. If the vital breath is there, you are there and so is Ishvara. In such simplified fashion, nobody has expounded this profound knowledge.«
- Nisargadatta Maharaj; ›Ultimate medicine‹ -

ABHYASA of PRATYAHARA
or
moving into stillness

»What is called mind is a wondrous power residing in the Self.
It causes all thoughts to arise. Apart from thoughts there is no such thing as mind.
Therefore thought is the nature of mind.«
- Ramana Marharshi; ›Who am I? Nan Yar‹, ›8‹ -

»The mind moves in certain channels and grooves. I have seen that the sentiments or
emotions or feelings are a channel through which it expresses itself in one way.
The thought is another channel. These are organized channels through which the mind
expresses; so every day the expression will be different, obviously every moment it
will be different but I have seen that all the emotion and sentiments put together and
all the thoughts, noble or ignoble put together, is only a cerebral way of behaviour.«
- Vimala Thakar; ›Talks in Australia‹ 1977, p.157 -

Intro

Asana, Pranayama & Pratyahara as right personal (physical, vital & mental) evolution,
cultivate the space for transpersonal involution. From mental conception to transmental
perception; from stillness to silence ... where the meditative and absorptive flow of *Dhyana*
takes us back to the source of our Being – *the path of pratiprasava or the ›return to the
source‹* (Y.S.2.10&11).

In Pratyahara we link personal evolution and transpersonal involution through the
personic aspect of *sens(e)ual stillness* and the cosmic aspect of *mindful awareness.* Having
refined body & breath through the qualities of stability & dynamic, now in Pratyahara *we
let the quality of stillness* refine the *mind.* In its personic aspect *Pratyahara* is the personal
practice of *stillness* to sense and transcend the *mental* mind or *manas.* In its cosmic aspect
Pratyahara pertains to the transpersonal practice of *silence,* that is still awareness of our
mindful mind or *Chitta,* the totality of personal consciousness.

Pratyahara is the practice of **Abhyasa** *(right effort)* itself, which together with **Vairagya**
(right attitude) & **Viveka** *(right understanding)* constitute the accomplished stages of yogic
endeavour and are the inspiration and destination for our personal practices of Asana,
Mudra & Pranayama.

Pratyahara is therefore the involutionary essence of the evolutionary practices of Asana,
Mudra & Pranayma. As the evolutionary process of *Abhyasa* ripens and bears fruit in the
unfoldment of *Vairagya* and arising *Viveka,* so does the practice of Asana, Mudra &
Pranayama bear fruit in the unfoldment of Pratyahara and arising mindfulness. *What
Vairagya is to Abhyasa, Pratyahara is to Asana and Pranayama.*

**Once we are established in body, space & breath through Asana, Mudra & Pranayama,
Mudra will integrate and dissolve two-directional into Asana and Pranayama by giving
structural dynamic to the former and pranic stability to the latter. Thus we evolve from
Asana, Mudra & Pranayama to Asana, Pranayama & Pratyahara, the essential practice of
body, breath & mind!**

... on Pratyahara ...

The practices of Asana, Mudra & Pranayama prepare and refine body & breath for personal (*stable & dynamic*) unfolding, free from (and for) identity with *activity and feeling.* The practice of Pratyahara prepares and refines *stillness* within the sense-crowded mind and frees us from (and for) identity with *thought.*

Pratyahara then becomes synonymous with *right effort* and expresses itself through *dhyana,* freeing us from (and for) identity with our fluctuate personality at large through *chitta vritti nirodha.* (The perfected practice of Pranayama resulting in *prana vritti nirodha* is synonymous with chitta vritti nirodha but difficult to reach without extended guidance from a true Hatha Guru).

Done with pride and strive, Asana and Pranayama further deepen the conditions and bounds of our habituated personality, becoming obstacles in themselves and missing the point of revealing the person. Do we get the ease of bodily well-being or attachment to physical beauty and fancy postures?
Do we get pranic awareness and breath-expansion or retentive oxygen kicks?
Do we transcend afflictions of body & breath or do we perpetuate and refine our ego?
Do we arrive at Pratyahara with the dynamic stability of space, empty and receptive for the internal journey to unfold or do we arrive loaded with conceptual baggage of how proceedings should be?

A sophisticated Pranayama practice includes **Pratyahara** *and enables us for* **Dharana.**
A sophisticated Pratyahara practice includes **Dharana** *and enables us for* **Dhyana.**

Pratyahara is the most subtle aspect of personal practice. It is a fine tuning of body & breath, cultivating *mental* stability, dynamic & stillness – *clarity.*

Part 1

manomaya or the myth of the mind

Body & breath are graspable entities, while the *mind* evades our grasping by being essentially a balanced coordination of the former two. Likewise also *Asana & Pranayama* appear as accessible techniques, while *Pratyahara* is too subtle and actually more a fine-tuning of the former, than an independent practice in itself.

As the gross body can be inquired through Asana & Mudra and even the fine breath is accessible enough to be inquired into with Mudra & Pranayama, the mind seems to be too subtle for direct access and inquiry. And so does an actual practice of *Pratyahara* evade a clearcut structure. The still practice of Pratyahara is a harmonious interplay of stability-body & dynamic-breath through their practical aspects of Asana & Pranayama.
In the same line also *thought,* far too subtle for direct access, is factually an outcrop of *sensation & emotion* – as well as their maintainer and source.

As Asana in all its variety always has the body as focus and reference point and Pranayama always has the breath, *Pratyahara* evades such a point since its necessary mental or sens(e)ual stability depends upon the interplay of body & breath. What happens to the *mind,* once we start to understand body & breath, also happens to *Pratyahara* once we start to understand Asana & Pranayama ... *the evading factor!!* It dissolves into the harmonious interdependence of body & breath.

As an ever demanding entity the mind exists because of friction between body & breath. Body & breath in equanimity mean the annihilation of the roving mind which otherwise feeds and perpetuates itself by sens(e)ualising and blowing up what originally was only a symptom of an aggravated body-breath condition.
Thus the thinking or mental mind is the inevitable outcrop of body-breath friction, that means *thought* stirs itself up through the friction of *sensation & emotion* and becomes their source and destiny. *Solving this vritti-friction is to dissolve the mental mind which then has served its purpose!*

Pratyahara as collected mindfulness arises once the friction of Asana (sensation-body) & Pranayama (emotion-breath) dissolve. As long as there is an active practice of Pratyahara its emphasis is either asanic or pranayamic. The moment Pratyahara sets in is the moment of harmonic and frictionless body-breath-happening: *asanic* Pranayama or *pranayamic* Asana; structural vitality or vital structure; stable dynamic or dynamic stability. *The apparent body-mind duality merges into a tridal understanding of integral body-breath-mind unity.*

When body & breath are harmoniously interacting, the mind expresses itself through the translation of existential urges and intuitive insights, providing the existential and creative survival on an individual level. This is the original space of the mind, to serve as a functional and inspirational element.

>»When a healthy body and vital breath (prana) function together, the sense of
beingness expresses itself by putting into operation the limbs and senses of the body.«
> - Nisargadatta Maharaj; ›The nectar of immortality‹, p.88 -

Part 2

mind, senses & perception

Since the mind is the seat of perception, the senses can stay either within perceiving internal or move without perceiving external phenomena. Our perception of the outside world happens inside the head. Since the recognition of the sense-organs do not happen in the ears, skin, eyes, mouth or nose but in the mind their chief organ, the whole outer perception is to be found there. The senses don't have any preference and magnetise towards whatever space accommodates and facilitates them. As Sw. Vivekananda says: *»Sense perception is an inference and yet all inference comes from sense perception.«*

The nature of this world is to exist through change. There is no way to stop this world from existing and changing. No way to stop the movements of the mind and to live in this world. The mind can be harnessed, channelled, directed and even understood but it can not be stopped. The yogic effort of controlling and restricting the mental flow is not to stop it but *to step out and cessate ones identity with it.*

It is the egoic self-perpetuating principle inherent in the mind that blows up percieved phenomena into nonsense desires and aversions and identifies with them. It invades the spacious capacity for stillness and drives the silence of sense-perception out into the noise of sense-conception. Once that space is reclaimed, the senses spontaneously recollect themselves back at their source.

Misusing and taking advantage of our personal dilemma of knowing the senses as the perciever of their objects but not knowing what percieves the senses in the first place, the egoic mind is able to perpetuate and blow itself up to such an extent that it invades and occupies the whole space of mindfulness in which plain perception could happen and simple recognition would take place. *Thus pushed out into the world of concepts and conditions, the senses pervert their original function of unconditioned and unqualified perception.*

»Knowing the relative field of utility of the mind and brain; using it precisely and
accurately in that field and letting it alone
when we know that it cannot proceed any further, is the proper way.«

»To let go the mind, where the activity of mind is not relevant. The mind and its
activities are relevant to certain fields of activities, certain areas, where we have to
operate through mind. But the whole cerebral structure having been conditioned in a
number of ways, is not capable of perceiving the totality of existence.«
- Vimala Thakar; ›Totality in essence‹ -

Part 3

more on Pratyahara

At the level of Pratyahara our sense-perceived personality of sensation, emotion & thought temporarily dissolves into its own withdrawal, with the arising mental stillness serving as a reference point for our *sense of beingness* (chittasyasvarupa, Y.S.2.54). This temporary dissolution of the superficial or mental mind provides a scenic background for arising awareness of our higher or mindful Mind. Though the nature of this ›higher‹ Mind (being the link to the Self) is quite mysterious, it is intuitively felt or sensed and we can project this sense as an *image of the Self (sense of beingness)* onto the screen of *stable mental stillness.* It will include all other senses as long as we can stay with it (Y.S.2.55).

Then the senses are recollected within and prevented from going out by holding on to that feel-able but not traceable *sense of beingness* (mindfulness). As long as we are submerge with this primal sense, the mind stays within and keeps the other senses self-abiding at home in their respected places or spaces – *the art of abidance and being still.*

Stillness makes us empty. The empty mind is passive, spacious and able to recieve without getting loaded. Ambitious mental efforts fill this space up and block awareness, mindfulness and even concentration from arising. *The pratyaharic sense-withdrawal dissolves the conceptual mental mind into a perceptual mindful one.*

»Hence forcing the mind into silence and stimulating chemically or neurotically a state
of quietness in the mind, is not a spontaneous cessation of mental activity,
and no further enquiry can take place unless one arrives at the spontaneous cessation
of total mental activity out of understanding the mind«
- Vimala Thakar; ›Totality in Essence‹, p.22/3 -

... letting stillness happen and presence arise ...

The emptiness of mind becomes the fullness of awareness – void of mental conception and full of conscious perception. To draw our senses within, we collect our mind in stillness: **Be still and know that I am**. The practice of Pratyahara is therefore the effort to reverse the direction of the outdriven senses and to regain, reclaim and reestablish their original internal space. *Being still, letting presence arise, we are in Pratyahara – merging the mind into the silence of the moment.*

We move into Pratyahara with the long–subtle *(dirgha-sukshma)* pranayamic breath, with the mudric attention shifted from bodily onto mental space; the place of our deepest sense or feeling of *beingness.* Having established this attentive link we resolve the breath back into its own natural mode. It is a simple abiding in abidance and whenever lost a coming back to it. Loosing Pratyahara time and again because of its subtility we move back into the ease of steady breathing *(sthira-sukha* of the pranayamic body) and try again.

Since Pratyahara represents stillness or mental stability the subtle aspect of our personality, it will take practical time to establish a certain efficiancy and routine in it – again and again wading through old patterns in ever new disguises. Our mental fickleness needs to understand itself by being reflected on moments of stillness, due to a reconciled body-breath.

If our practice is ambitious and expectant, it will be difficult to cultivate Pratyahara; if our practice is self-contained &-content, Pratyahara will be the natural outcome. The establishment of Pratyahara is the furthest we can refine our threefold person – *the physical body, the vital breath and their mental space.* It is the practical touchstone for personal integrity. *The practice of the* **mind** *is the refinement of harmonising* **body & breath** *and therefore also their essence and destination.*

... evolving & resolving ...

As Asana & Pranayama resolve in Pratyahara, sensation & emotion resolve in thought. Likewise the stability of the body and the dynamic of the breath resolve in mental stillness and the person evolves in Silence. As the two dissolve in the third, all three resolve in all-pervading conscious awareness, the totality of our Being. As body, breath & mind dissolve in the person, the person resolves in the Self. *The mind is either lost in thoughts or to be found in the Self.* Evolved Abhyasa culminates in ›chitta-vritti-nirodha‹ and is synonymous with meditation. Here and then we have the chance to temporarily drop the burden or veil of our persona and let the light of the Self genuinely reflect and shine.

... cosmic conclusion ...

As the macrocosmic universal correlates to our microcosmic individual, we have the opportunity to link our personal individuality with cosmic universality – with the always bigger picture. *Mahat* (universal intelligence) the second *tattvic* or prakritic principle evaporating intuitively out of the worldground and pervading cosmic space, becomes for *purushic (atma-ic)* reasons individualised, personalised and is ›limiting‹ itself as Buddhi (individual intelligence) into *Chitta,* the conscious web of our person. *Pratyahara is the personal recognition of this ›limitation‹ and the doorway to re-access our original and limitless cosmic intuitive intelligence-potential.*

»I believe that the stillness of Pratyahara has a special attractive power ... and I am
telling you, reader, not as a teacher from the eminence of bliss attained, but
as a fellow traveller in the dust of the road to the temple of the undistracted Mind.«
- F. Yeats-Brown -

 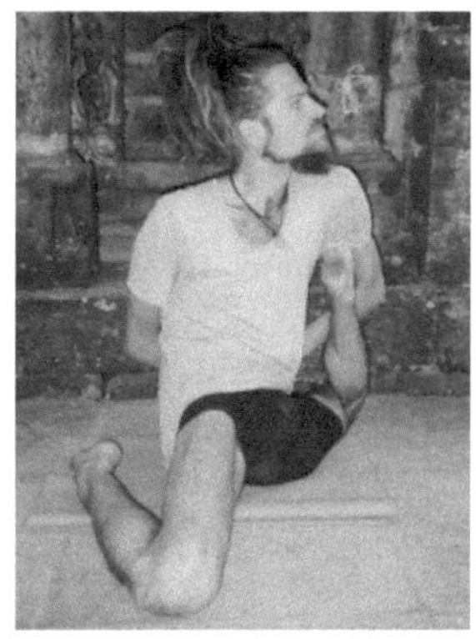

VAIRAGYA of NI-YAMA
or
lived Ni-Yamas, the ashtangic destination

»Man commits certain deeds, he practices certain things. You cannot stop him.
His nature will compel him to act. He cannot stop himself. Well, I can stop myself for
some time by my intellectual forces, but nature will not pardon me. There are certain
natural expressions in man and those he has got to express, now or a little later.
He cannot help it. Because of your intellectual environment, you have come to
understand that you should not speak this way, you should not act that way, but this is
suppression and at some point it is going to explode the entire life. As a result
of this the evolution of the soul will be retarded. In order to speed up the evolution of
the soul, the best thing is to let the soul function freely.«
- ›Early teachings of Sw.Satyananda Saraswati‹; B.S.Y. Munger 1967/88, p.284 -

Intro

Vairagya is the cultivation of right attitude and *Ni-Yamas* are its living expression. Vairagya signifies the essential attitude necessary for all yogic paths, be it karm-ic, bhakt-ic or jnan-ic: the ability to give our best without creating expectations or attachments. The effort of *Abhyasa* and the letting go of *Vairagya* will eventually lead to the wisdom of arising *Viveka*. Abhyasa is the key to unlock Vairagya. It is the purity of Abhyasa which brings forth Vairagya. It is the integrity of Vairagya which keeps Abhyasa pure. We commence our practice with abhyasic effort and arising Vairagya is our attitudal check. *Vairagya is the practice of attitude and expresses herself in niyamic personal integration and yamic social behaviour.*

It is similar with *Yama & Niyama.* While to a certain degree *Yamas,* as social behaviour, can be actively pursued, like trying not to harm, lie or be greedy, it is also a limited approach as most of our behaviour happens not from a volitional and aware state of mind, but from a habituated and conditioned one. Usually it is only afterwards that we realise how we have acted or behaved. The *Niyamas,* as personal behaviour, are even less possible to be directly pursued and practiced. They express themselves symptomatically through personal maturity and integrity, which is the goal rather than the means of our endeavour.

The vairagyic motto ›to be detached from things seen or heard‹ (Y.S. 1.15) is the best yamic condition not to violate, lie, steal, misuse or covet. And it is the ›content detachment towards experience in its whole range‹ (Y.S.1.16), which keeps us pure or niyamic. We accomplish *Vairagya* through *abhyasic* understanding and maturity, which expresses in assimilated *ni-yamic* values.

Patanjali denotes 16 Sutras (2.30-45) to the exposition of *Yama & Niyama* and considering the terseness of his work, the amount of attention he attributes to them shows that these universal and individual values have indeed an existential and essential character, rather than being merely preparatory moral stages. Quite on the contrary they seem to be the *ashtangic* destination, with the following six *angas* (limbs) serving as specific means to bring about *ni-yamic* mastery. *They are the source and destiny of our ashtangic unfoldment!*

So instead of squeezing the Ni-Yamas into *Bahiranga* (external first five limbs of ashtanga) and thus reducing them to be mere beginner lessons and moral incentives, they represent an own integrity – *Vairagya* – and reveal once more the way of the trinity:

NI-YAMAS	BAHIRANGA	ANTARANGA
Attitude	Effort	Insight
Vairagya	Abhyasa	Viveka

Part 1

YAMA

... the great vows ...

The Yamas point out the need for social behaviour since as human beings we are all interrelated and even more so interdependent. Yamas express our need to live as an individual in the universal; with the personic split between ›within & without‹, ›the me & the other‹. Until this enigma between me and the world is sufficiently experienced understood, and transcended, we will have to recognise and accept external or yamic values which need to be acknowledged and adhered to in order to enable and maintain ourselves within humanity.

The *harmlessness* of **Ahimsa** needs the *truth* of **Satya,** includes the *non-stealing & non-greediness* of **Asteya** & **Aparigraha** and expresses itself in the cont(in)ent *integrity* of roving **Brahmacharya.** *Aparigraha* is the non-reception of superfluous, or unnecessary things and gifts vested with interest, which may block our independent perception and action. *Brahmacharya* in its truest sense means ›*moving in brahmic mastery*‹ or in that delightful state which never turns into its opposite as all common enjoyments do sooner or later ... *bliss is.*

Introducing the *Yamas* (Y.S.2.30), Patanjali immediately points out in the next Sutra their uncompromising authority in form of the great vows or *mahavrata.* Thus he is taking away any doubts or wishful thoughts about exceptions and modifications. Not to kill might seem reasonable (including the mosquito issue) but not to violate or harm in speech or thought is on a different footing. The Yamas are universally self-explaining and after ascerting their uncompromisable validity, more emphasis is given on describing their extraordinary attainments than on the means to reach them – the *Siddhis* of the *Yamas:* no enmity, verbal power, spontaneous enrichment, vigorous courage, existential knowledge (Y.S.2.35-39).

Unlike the Niyamas which are unescapable, the Yamas are. Not breaking by evading them does not serve the purpose for their accomplishment. Living in seclusion or solitude for longer or shorter periods to probe deeply into our nature, will give us little opportunity to go against them. We may choose those conditions temporarily to facilitate our abhyasic engagement but not to accomplish yamic integration, which can be verified only in the social context of harmonious living. *Yamas as external pointers and Niyamas as internal direction; together they express vairagyic unfoldment and integrity.*

As we are always in the personal relationship with body, breath & mind and do continuously act, feel & think, it depends on the depth of our yogic maturity how asanic,
pranayamic or pratyaharic those expressions are. Similar it is with the body of the Yamas
expressing age-old universal values which in one way or the other always were existent
and are ingrained in our humane psyche. It depends on the depth of our yamic integrity
how able and free we can live up to them. As they are essentially interdependent, each one
will express evenly in all. We can't develop or neglect one without developing or neglec-
ting the others ... *one for all and all for one!*

As the major part of the third *pada* (chapter) in the Y.S. is concerned with the attainments of the various accomplished *Samyamas,* so also in the second *pada* there is ample
space given for the attainments of the accomplished *Ni-Yamas.* S.S.Varma's statement
in his book ›Yogic practice‹ (Adyar library 2002, p.8) about Ahimsa actually goes for
all the Yamas: they »really denote(s) an attitude and mode of behaviour towards all
living creatures based on the recognition of the underlying unity of life. As spirituality
is based on the doctrine of the One Life, outer behaviour must conform to this all-
embracing law of life. If this principle is understood thoroughly, its application in life
will become much easier.«

Part 2

NIYAMA

From ›*cheerful purity – mastery over the body and its senses – one-pointedness – possible
vision of the Self – unexcelled joy – communion with ones chosen divinity*‹ up to ›*perfection
in Samadhi*‹, all is potentially ingrained in the practice of the Niyamas as described in the
Y.S.2.40-45. The whole yogic quest seems to be contained and content within their realm,
as is rightly said by Mikel Burley: »The body must be purified for Yoga to occur, yet Yoga
is itself the purifying process« (›Hatha-Yoga‹; Motilal Banarsidass, Delhi 2000, p.132).

... pratipaksha bhavana & chitta prasadana ...

Having explained the Yamas and their universality, Patanjali moves on to the Niyamas which are individual in character. They are neither positive as in affirmations (be honest), nor negative as in prohibitions (don't lie); but creative attitudal challenges – be pure, content, effortful, investigative & dedicated – and therefore need a supportive advice rather than an authorative statement. This support is given as *pratipaksha bhavana* or the cultivation of opposittes (Y.S. 2.33 & 34) which means, that to free us from unwholesome thought, we need to develop its complementary and wholesome contrariness.

To believe in the importance of dealing with unkind thoughts by opposing them with loving kindness is one thing, to actually internalise and truly feel that loving kindness is quite another and demands a lot of understanding. To cultivate such a refined mentality (the peaceful mind of *chitta-prasadana),* Patanjali gives us the clue in Y.S.1.33 where he describes the right attitude to our environment in general: ›to be friendly with happiness; compassionate with unhappiness; joyful with the virtuos; indifferent with the non-virtuos.‹

The mind checking on itself is treading a fine line and can easily slip into the phenomena described by Ramana Maharshi, as »the thief who takes on the uniform of the police man, pretending to catch the thief«. *Pratipaksha bhavana* is not a mental reasoning of good over bad but expresses the deep seated conviction that life is essentially unitive, wholesome and all-embracive. We tell the truth not because we believe lying is bad but because there is no incentive in us which makes us want to tell a lie.

The reason given for the need of *pratipaksha-bhavana & chitta-prasadana* is that negative thoughts, emotions or actions, however justified they seem to be, will inevitable end up in *dukha and ajnana* (suffering and nescience (Y.S.2.34)). Embracing life with a ›friendly, compassionate, joyful or indifferent‹ outlook will cultivate and pacify our mentality, lessen our ignorant urge and may manifest as Niyama and express as Yama.

The general impersonal and impassionate character of the Y.S. offer with 1.33 & 2.33/34 two very personal and compassionate practices. It would be futile to argue that Patanjali copied them from buddhist thought because being so compact and terse (and of course buddhist) in nature, there isn't any space for cross-philosophical references or comparison in his exposition. Rather those practices seem to be essential for imbibing the yogic process.

Kriya

... self-practice, self-study & Self-dedication ...

It is remarkable that Patanjali as well as Hatha-Yoga find the origin of *Kriya* in the Niyamas. As Yamas keep us sane in the world, Niyamas show the conditions necessary for the inner journey back to the source – the *Self.* If these conditions are sensibly cultivated, all yogic practices fall into place and express living Niyamas in a yamic world ... *this expression or process is the dynamic of Kriya.*

The preparatory practices *(Shat-kriya)* of the Hatha-Yogi trace themselves back to the Niyamas of *Saucha and Tapa;* and the *Kriya-Yoga* of Patanjali constitutes the last three Niyamas of *Tapa, Svadhyaya & Ishvarapranidhana.* The common ground is the pure effort of *Tapa* and *Santosha,* the Niyama in between, implies the necessary content outlook essential for those practices. For without such a sustained sense of personal and natural contentment, it will be difficult to recognise ›suffering‹ *(dukha)* as ignorance and not as personal guilt or sin.

It seems obvious that the notion of *Kriya and Niyama* go together, since as long as we are not established in the state of Yoga we are unavoidably acting and doing something (including nothing) to either bring such a state about or to prevent other states from happening. This *kriya-ic* process primarily consists in the cultivation of *niyamic* values. The preparatory practice of *Kriya*-Yoga is therefore preparatory all the way until the bonds of *Avidya* or ignorance are cut and *Yoga* becomes the natural expression of our daily life.

As Yama helps to bring about Niyama, it is in the nature of Niyama to express through Yama: as harmlessness begets purity, purity is harmless. And as *ashtangic* techniques help to actualise *Kriya*-Yoga (the cultivation of *Samadhi* and the attenuation of *Kleshas,* Y.S.2.2), so it is in the nature of *Kriya*-Yoga to express itself through *ashtangic* techniques (culminating in revealing full *Viveka* or the faculty for discriminative awareness and intuitive insight, Y.S.2.28/29).

Part 3

Saucha - Purity (& Brahmacharya)

With the Niyama of *Saucha* we find a similar confusion as with the Yama of *Brahmacharya*. *Saucha* or purity, instead of seeing its independent, free and positive aspect not to become overly body-attached (with ones own and others), it is traditionally pushed into the negation of the body and into disgust towards self and others. The traditional translation of *jugupsa* (Y.S.2.40) as disgust towards the body as a result of *Saucha,* has rightly been clarified by Feuerstein in his book on the Yoga-Sutra (Inner Traditions India, 1989, p.86), who translates *jugupsa* as ›distance‹ to bodily notions instead of finding disgust in them.

Even so the result of *Brahmacharya* (›to move in and with the absolute‹) in the Yoga Sutras is *vigour & vitality, it is* traditionally understood as suppression and prohibition of sexual conduct ... and this suppression is then strangely supposed to unleash this vigourness and vitality. True enough we all have our personal store of mixed- and pent-up karmic energy within our psyche and trying to dissolve them with sexual obsessions is pouring kerosene into the fire and amplifies our confusion ... and remarkably not only since the *neo-sannyasic new age* but possibly since ancient vedic times.

It is the rightly understood *nirodha* (cessation) of frantic identity with the body which makes us pure & cont(in)ent. The arising wisdom of *Saucha* is to see the body as what it is: body – not more, not less, not judgeable. *Saucha* protects and distances us from cosmetic notions and judgments over ourselves and others.

In Yoga Sutra 2.41 the other and indeed amazing attainments of mastered *Saucha* are listed which are actually synonymic with Yoga in general! They are: the refined purity of *sattva-shuddhi* – the gladness of *saumanasya* – the one-pointedness of *ekagrata* – the sensuous mastery of *indriya-jaya* and the fitness or *yogyata* for *atma-darshana,* the vision of the Self. This explains amply why the Hatha-Yogis see *Saucha* as the root of their preparatory practices. Coming back to the connection with *Brahmarcharya,* it is certainly not sexual disgust which *Saucha* produces but the pure and innocent integration of the body into the person.

Santosha – Contentment

Whether we are bent towards the hatha-yogic approach rooted in *Saucha-Tapa* or towards the raja-yogic approach rooted in *Tapa-Svadhyaya-Ishvarapranidhana*, we need the essential quality of *Santosha* or contentment. Contentment with ourselves as we are and with life as it is and not as we wish or want it to be. Being content allows us to move steadily and sincere along our path without the empty need to excell or exhibit. No hankering after recognition and applause, certified authority or other hanky-panky. Being steadily content prevents us from becoming agitated or shallow when the intensity of life's mystic unfolds in the dilemma (of realising): that ultimately there is nothing to progress to but all we can do is progress – that the paths destination is reached by stillness but all we can do is move – that there are no concepts and techniques in and for the Absolute but yet we are choicelessly bound to them in our personal illusions – that there is nothing to do but all we can do is to do.

Contentment means to embrace our being with beingness; to embrace *that* with *what is*. It is a positive attitude towards life and oneself. The contentment of *Santosha* knows no opposite ... no excitement-depression movie. There is no surpressed resentment in content *Santosha* but a recognition of what we potentially are: essentially whole (and divine!) Santosha has the qualities of insistence, tolerance and endurance which need and procure content beingness. The attainment of *Santosha* is unsurpassed joy or *anuttama-sukha* (Y.S.2.42) and is unbound by the personic law of changing moods ... coming & going it doesn't leave bitter fruits.

Tapa - Svadhyaya - Ishvarapranidhana

Patanjali uses the threefold pattern of Kriya Yoga, which once understood, can be found underlying every aspect of life and its actions. This tridal pattern appears and is confirmed in all truth-seeking traditions, verbalising in various ways the mystery of the trinity: **Tapa,** the effort for outer *access* – **Svadhyaya,** the attitude for inner process – **Ishvara-pranidhana,** the unfoldment of progressive *success. The unfoldment of attitude through effort.*

Staying within the cultural context of ancient yogic-vedic heritage, Patanjali employs these terms in their antique brahmanic nomenclature and thus takes away the chance to modify or qualify them due to fashionable desires of our vain complacent ways. Dry to the bone but also as compact and supportive as those, they are the skelleton which we enflesh with the maturing understanding of our yogic practice.

These Niyamas are so deeply inter-connected that it is more revealing to see them in context as in Patanjali's definition of Kriya-Yoga. As Niyama they pertain to our attitude and as Kriya they pertain to our practice. To see the depth of each one we need the context of the other two. The Tapa of *Svadhyaya* culminates and fructifies in Ishvarapranidhana. **Svadhyaya** is the Tapa, which needs the dedicated resolution of *Ishvarapranidhana.* The divine truth of Svadhyaya shines forth through the *Tapa* of **Ishvarapranidhana.**

... Tapa ...

Tapa, widely and wildly discussed, defined, rejected and insisted upon, stands for the need of ›external‹ effort through will. *The abhyasic path of outer access.* It is an establishment in the endeavour of burning our defilements. The heat (through the friction of effort) of Tapa can purify up to the point of bodily and sensory perfection, *Kaya- and Indriya-Siddhi* (Y.S.2.43). Compact and powerful as it is, we can link and connect with Tapa on many levels: *the effort of Abhyasa, Hatha, Asana, Karma – the need to do.*

... Svadhyaya ...

More subtle (and deceiving) the *Self-study* of *Svadhyaya* stands for the need of ›internal‹ effort to relate with our-Self. It is *the vairagyic path of inner process* through understanding and letting go. Traditionally understood as reflective and contemplative study of truth-bearing scriptures, it became in yogic commentaries an ›*om*-ing‹ discipline for one-pointedness through repetition and reflection on *Pranava* (the cosmic symbol pronounced as aum or om). Commencing with dedicated *jappa* or recitation of om – which is the classical practice of Ishvarapranidhana – we breathe or respirate into *ajappa* (unspoken recitation) of throat-sounding *so* (with the inhale) & *ham* (with the exhale), being the ongoing respirative ascertainment of ›He-I am‹. The *adhyaya* (knowing by heart) of ones *sva* (own) ... *where the heart knows the Self in the divine communion of Svadhyaya.*

According to the Yoga Sutra *Svadhyaya* results in direct communion with our *ishta-devata,* our chosen divine principle or personal divinity (Y.S.2.44). This *ishta*/chosen *devata*/ divinity (deriving from the root *div* ›to shine‹) denotes to that divine essence shining forth within us, which is in our nearest and dearest range of reach and expresses through the vital breath. Breathing ourselves to life and sustaining us with the direct communion between ›us & our*Self*‹.

... Ishvarapranidhana ...

Most subtle and delicate the dedication of *Ishvarapranidhana* stands for our inmost attitude. Once tapped it is unfolding divinity itself (as god, guru or Self) and the original primal cause which shapes our life and actions – the *vivekic path of progressive success.* It is our graceful potential for intuition and insight into to the source of our *Self.* Compared to the characteristic terseness of the Y.S., the concept of *Ishvara* gets defined at great length. Patanjali reveals *Ishvara* not as a creating-sustaining-transcending divinity or power, but as a special or ideal form of *Purusha* itself. With the essential difference that it never was or ever will be touched by *prakritic* identity and bondage (Y.S.1.24) ... *it is essentially free identity.*

The *ishvaric principle* serves as the highest and most precious refinement or attainment we can aspire to – the limitless limit, the potential potency ... the always bigger picture.

The mode of actual connection between us and *Ishvara* is one of ›cosmic sympathy‹ as M. Eliade puts it; a connection that differs in degrees of perception rather than in quality or essence.

Ishvarapranidhana does not perpetuate a belief system but an attitudal dedication and devotion towards the highest principle within us. In its light all attainments and achievements appear relative and petty and leave no other option than to humbly bow down to our personal *limitations* and *potentials*.

The yogic attainment of *Isvarapranidhana* is perfection of Samadhi or Samadhi-siddhi (Y.S.2.45), the goal of all goals. It is therefore also the highest form of *Abhyasa* and our *vairagyic* culmination and *vivekic* destination. Often theistically described, *Isvarapranidhana* pertains much more to our inner attitude and dedication than to an outer believe system; even the »atheistic« Buddhists revere highly the notion of *pranidhana* and the need for firm dedicated resolution in their path and practice of awakening.

It is sincerity and dedication which brings us to and also radiates through *Ishvarapranidhana*. The classical practice is *Svadhyaya* (om-jappa) and the effort is *Tapa*. The *tapasic* effort of Abhyasa and the *svadhyaya-ic* attitude of Vairagya flower in the vivekic revelation of the *ishvara* principle – *the divinity of the Self.*

... conclusion ...

The actual practice of Ishvarapranidhana is Svadhyaya and the effort needed is Tapa. This is the kriya-ic integration and destination of all the Yoga, symbolised through **Abyhasa, Vairagya & Viveka.** A practical and direct means for diminishing delusions and developing wisdom (Y.S.2.1-2). Cultivating the ›experience‹ of personal transcendence in *Samadhi,* culminating in a cloud of virtue or *dharma-megha,* which showers the lasting freedom of *Kaivalya* upon us (Y.S.4.29-30); the grand theme of the fourth *pada*/chapter in the Yoga Sutras.

Tapa is the motivating force behind Svadhyaya and ultimately behind Ishvarapranidhana. Neither superior nor inferior to each other, they are modes of access to establish the tridal pillar for emancipation. **Svadhyaya** is not intellectual satisfaction of our mental capacity, but a one-pointed ›om-going‹ inquiry into our Self and the journey towards. **Ishvarapranidhana** is not a refuge under religious authority and subjugation but an unfolding recognition of the divine cosmic potential within us. It is the solar brightness of this recognition that makes us humble and bow down to the firm dedication of *pranidhana.*

To make it plain that Yoga practice aims more at the *bliss* of right attitude, than at the *high* of technical extacy, Patanjali puts the concept of Kriya into the *niyamic*/attitudal fold. Empowered by the *purity of contentment* and expressed through the *Yamas.*

yogic trinities

Body	Breath	Mind
Abhyasa	Vairagya	Viveka
Tapa	Svadhyaya	Ishvarapranidhana
Karma	Bhakti	Jnana
Effort	Letting go	Insight
Access	Process	Success

Why does the devotion of *Bhakti* corresponds to the Self-study of *Svadhyaya* and the gnostic state of *Jnana* to the devotional resolution of *Ishvarpranidhana?* Like *Vairagya & Viveka,* so also *Bhakti & Jnana* are attitudal and intuitive unfoldings, resulting from right practice (Abhyasa) and action (Karma). They are outside our direct volitional reach and thus also outside of a clearcut definition and they are interrelated and complementary principles.

Svadhyaya or the establishment of a (knowing) relationship with our own Self requires dedication and devotion. This self-contact of *Svadhyaya* needs the attitudal purity of *Bhakti. Ishvarapranidhana* or the dedication towards the highest principle within requires discerning knowledge and perception. The resolution of *Ishvarapranidhana* correlates thus with the knowledge of *Jnana.*

In our yogic unfoldment it is *Bhakti* that produces *Jnana* when understood and it is *Jnana* that produces *Bhakti* when devoted. *Bhakti is Jnana and Jnana is Bhakti, the access is Karma.*

»Without the vital breath, Ishwara or God has no soul; and without God
the vital breath has no existence. Whenever man limits his consciousness to body and
mind, he is called jiva. Otherwise he is absolutely
independent of these two, which are acting and reacting.«
- Nisargadatta Maharaj; ›The ultimate medicine‹ -

»The systematic cultivation of faith, devotion and love (without blind superstition
and fanatical bigotry or narrowness) involves the practice of pratyahara,
dharana and dhyana and may, if earnestly pursuit lead to the attainment of
samadhi and the spiritual illumination of the whole being.«
- A.K. Banerjea; ›The philosophy of Goraknath‹, p.15 -

VIVEKA of SAMYAMA
or
the discerning path of insight

>»In the nondualistic expirience the knower, knowledge and knowable become one.
Thus he who knows Brahman becomes Brahman ...
In Samadhi the meditator, meditation and the object of meditation,
all these three become one. This is the culmination of vedantic realization«
- Commentaries on the ›Avadhuta Gita‹ (1.1&12); Sw. Chetananda, Ramakrishna Mission -

Intro

Having cultivated *abhyasic effort* and *vairagyic attitude,* we tune into the dimension of *Viveka,* its *discernment, insight and wisdom.* Through the effort of Abhyasa we sharpen our personality and through the detachment of Vairagya we are not swayed or distracted by its tendencies. With the discriminative practice of *Viveka* we pierce straight into the heart of matters – *the thing as it is* – cutting through clouds and layers of our personal ignorance and habitual conditionings.

SAMYAMA

A practical expression for *Viveka* is *Samyama* (Y.S.3.4-6). *Samyama is the threefold constraint or tridal integration of concentrative Dharana, absorptive Dhyana and enstatic Samadhi.* The *stable* concentration of Dharana flows into *dynamic* absorption of Dhyana and reveals the *still* identity of enstatic Samadhi. Merged thus into a single process *Samyama* is used as a practical application to investigate into the true nature of things: *Prakriti & Purusha* (Y.2.18-23).

To comprehend through practice the deep interconnection and complementarity of *stability, dynamic & stillness* induces the transition from the *personal* to the *transpersonal.* Our continuous engagement with Abhyasa provides the screen which reflects our moody, changing and transient personality ... *the prakritic movie of gunatic fluctuation.* This reflecting may give us the necessary conviction to not overly identify with the petty phenomena arising and passing within our personality.

In Y.S.3.4, Patanjali expounds *Samyama* as ›trayam (Dharana, Dhyana, Samadhi) ekatra (in one) samyamaha (are Samyama)‹, presupposing of course that they are done on the same object. Patanjali is also careful to point out (Y.S.3.6) that the application of *Samyama* unfolds gradual and in stages (viniyoga). To avoid comparative expectations about internal experiences, he repeatedly states that the unfoldment of samadhic insight and wisdom happens in various states and stages and appear to be external or internal, seedy or seedless depending on our personal capacity and impersonal development (Y.S.2.27 & 3.6-8). By doing so he gives us the space to progress in our own individual cosmic-karmic rhythm, taking away the mental fixation of having to arrive somewhere at sometime.
Scholastic and academic definitions for this gradual process have been later added and commented upon. There are no set and fixed indicators for the unfoldment of insight and wisdom, maturity and freedom apart from our personal assimilation and natural expression of *ni-yamic* values ... which individually takes very different shapes.

SAMAPATTI

Leaving therefore the various stages of Samyama, the sevenfold unfoldment of wisdom and the seeded and unseeded Samadhis aside and up to transpersonal experience, we investigate into Samyama along the cognitive pattern of *Samapatti,* which is the technical term describing the samyamic process. **Sam***(together)*+**a***(unto)*+**patti***(falling):* Process of *complete merging – absorption – identity – falling into place – coincidence – coalescence – conclusion.*

»Samapatti means ›complete absorption‹, which is the positive result of Dhyana. After the fusion of the three aspects of cognition, there is total absorption of the individual consciousness in Samyama. This total absorption is the key which opens the door of Samadhi, because until and unless this absorption takes place there can be no experience of Samadhi. Only when samapatti is attained will the vision of the self manifest naturally and spontaneously, without any process of the individual consciousness.«
- ›Yoga Darshan‹ B.S.Y.; Sw. Niranjananda Saraswati, p.202 -

Samapatti is the yogic process outlined in Y.S.1.41: »When the vrittis have dwindled to a sufficient extent, the *Chitta* becomes pure and transparent like a jewel and is able to crystal-clear reflect without getting stained the true nature (svarupa) of any object coming within its sphere«.
This happens by merging or fusing objective cognition:

grahitr-grahana-grahya
cogniser-cognising-cognised
grasper-grasping-grasped
perceiver-percieving-percieved
knower-knowing-known
meditator-meditating-meditation
subject-verb-object.

Such tridal patterns underlie every cognitive experience and *Samapatti* is the means to let those patterns *fall into place, coalesce* and *conclude.* In the constraint of Samyama this process arises as concentration *(Dharana),* absorption *(Dhyana)* and completion *(Samadhi):*
In the *stable* process of *Dharana,* the ›grasper‹ binds its concentration onto the chosen object.
In the *dynamic* process of *Dhyana,* the ›grasping‹ is the meditative flow of absorbing the object.
In the *still* process of *Samadhi,* the ›grasped‹ object shines forth in its complete form or *svarupa,* pure cognition remains, revealing true perception.

Through the art of *Nirodha* (right cessation of wrong identity) and the dwindling of the *Vrittis* arises *Samapatti* as a ›falling into place‹ of our *vivekic* (Y.S.2.26-28; 3.52-54; 4.26-29) endeavour. It is the base for *samadhic* evolution and *samyamic* ability and rather than envisaging *Samapatti, Samadhi* or *Samyama* as means or goals in themselves, we experience them as spontaneous expressions. *Viveka unfolds as arising Samyama, which is the vairagyic expression of our abhyasic engagement.*

»If you see a little light, if you hear some sound, if you perceive a little truth, if you
have a glimpse of reality, that reality itself does not interest you;
but having seen that reality becomes a terrific issue and your mind converts it into a
tremendous experience, to be stored in memory, to be proud of, to be vain about;
and then you are more interested in telling people how you feel about the experience
than actually being in immediate contact with that reality.«
- Vimala Thakar; ›Blossoms of friendship‹, p.88 -

»The practice of concentration on breathing (anapanasati) is one of the well known
exercises, connected with the body, for mental development (bhavana).
There are several other ways of developing attentiveness in relation to the body as
modes of meditation. ... after a certain period you will expirience just that
split second, when your mind is fully concentrated on your breathings, when you will
not hear even sounds nearby, when no external world exists for you ...
that is the moment when you lose yourself completely in your mindfulness of breathing.
As long as you are conscious of yourself, you can never concentrate
on anything. This exercise of mindfulness of breathing, which is one of the simplest
and easiest practises, is meant to develop concentration up to very high
mystical attainments (dhyanas). Besides, the power of concentration is essential for any
kind of deep understanding, penetration, insight into the nature
of things, including the realization of nirvana.«
- Walpola Rahula ›What the Buddha taught‹ -

The Prajna Paramita Heart Sutra

When the Bodhisatva Avalokiteshvara
was coursing in the deep Prajna Paramita,
he perceived that all five Skandhas are empty.
Thus he overcame all ills and suffering.

Oh Sariputra, form does not differ from the void,
and the void does not differ from form.
Form is void and void is form;
the same is true for feelings,
perceptions, volitions and consciousness.

Sariputra, the characteristics of
the voidness of all Dharmas
are non-arising, non-ceasing, non-defiled,
non-pure, non-increasing, non-decreasing.

Therefore, in the void there are no forms,
no feelings, perceptions, volitions or consciousness.

No eye, ear, nose, tongue, body or mind;
no form, sound, smell, taste, touch or mind object;
no realm of the eye,
until we come to no realm of consciousness.

No ignorance and also no ending of ignorance,
until we come to no old age and death and
no ending of old age and death.

Also, there is no truth of suffering,
of the cause of suffering,
of the cessation of suffering, nor of the path.

There is no wisdom, and there is no attainment whatsoever.

Because there is no obstruction, he has no fear,
and he passes far beyond confused imagination,
and reaches ultimate Nirvana.

The Buddhas of the past, present and future,
by relying on Prajna Paramita,
have attained supreme enlightenment.

Therefore, the Prajna Paramita is the great magic spell,
the spell of illumination, the supreme spell,
which can truly protect one from all suffering without fail.

Therefore he uttered the spell of Prajnaparamita,
saying ›Gate, Gate, Paragate, Parasamgate, Bodhi Svaha‹.

(Translated into English by Venerable Dharma Master Lok To)

Quotes

**»It is in the nature of being to seek adventure in becoming,
as it is in the very nature of becoming to seek peace in being.«**
- Nisargadatta Maharaj; I am That-

Vimala Thakar

quoted from: ›Totality in essence‹ – ›Blossoms of friendship‹ – ›Talks in Australia.‹

»Everyday life is the only opportunity to live; and living means relating
to that which is.«

»In the human relationship is our opportunity to set ourselves free of the authority of
the mind, authority of knowledge and to relax in the innocence of intelligence.«

»A motiveless inquiry has no utility. Therefore it cannot be exploited.
It is the arrogance of the self, the me, the I, the ego, going out to acquire something in
the name of liberation, satori or mediation, that gets exploited.«

»Be concerned with the honesty, the integrity and the intensity of your own enquiry,
correlate it with all the life and leave the rest to life itself.«

»So when a person relates the inquiry to his total life, or rather relates his whole way
of living to that inquiry, then a very significant change becomes noticeable.«

»That is why I use the term ›inner order‹. Inner order is the result of your spontaneous action out of understanding; discipline is something that you force upon yourself
because the intellect accepts an idea. The intellect accepts an idea, the brain forces it
upon the physical structure and so there is resistance and irritation and friction, and
you have a sense of being imprisoned in the discipline. You feel as if you are a prisoner
out of your own mind, of your own brain, of your own intellect.«

»So long as we perceive through the sense organs, as long as we react through the
brain, we will see life divided into personality and impersonality,
tangibility and intangibility, the known and the unknown.
But there is a way of perceiving non-cerebrally. There is a way of direct and
immediate contact with reality. Perception born of non-duality and response born
of spontaneity, that is to live in God, that is to live in the awareness of life.«

»It's a very daring thing to say that the whole human psyche is very subtle matter, and
yet I say that consciousness, whether conditioned or unconditioned, is matter.«

»As long as man does not get acquainted with the invisible cerebral organ, as long as
he does not understand the mechanism of mind,
it is nearly impossible to arrive at the state of meditation.«

»What we do is, we claim to be sadhakas for some time of the day and claim to
be ordinary people for some other times of the day;
this inner contradiction must come to an end.«

»Movement and energy are the properties of matter.
Life is is-ness without any movement whatsoever.«

Nisargadatta Maharaj

quoted from: ›I am That‹, ›The ultimate medicine‹ & ›The nectar of immortality.‹

»You need not know to be, but you must be to know.«

»To know what you are, you must first investigate and know what you are not.»
»The whole object of the spiritual search or quest is to understand the concept as a
concept, the false as the false.«

»The main purpose of true spirituality is to liberate oneself completely
from one's concepts and conditionings ... in your true nature, you are the knower
of concepts and therefore prior to them.«

»Out of a common heap of wheat, many types of edibles are prepared, using different
methods. In the same way there are many systems of spirituality. I am not
interested in nibbling at the various delicacies – methods and techniques –
but only in the main course, which is the primordial source of all existence.«

»Because of the prana there is the mind. And because of the mind, there are the Vedas.
So ultimately, the source of this whole scripture is the vital force.
That is why I give full homage to the vital force.«

»The mind, which interprets happiness and unhappiness, is meant for
conducting the affairs of the world«

»M: You are before the mind is. Don't pay attention to the thoughts, pay attention to
the consciousness. Thoughts will always flow because of the vital breath.
Whatever thoughts are useful to you, you can make use of.«

»So you understand that your ›I-am-ness‹ or consciousness is there because of this
food body and because the vital breath is there. And you will be able to watch all these
elements: your body, the vital force and your beingness.
When you are in a position to watch all that, you get established in reality.«

»Who or what is the entity that is practising? Who is doing the sadhana?
It has no form and no shape. So what is it? It is within this form, this body –
the indwelling principle.
For how long will it continue practising? And what is the aim?
The aim is to abide in the self only. Until then it will continue the sadhana.«

»When anyone tells you to do some sadhana, with what can you do sadhana of any
kind? It can only be this life force. The only instrument one has to do sadhana with is
the life force. This life force, instead of viewing it merely as an instrument, has to be
treated – mentally accepted – as the highest principle in the world: that is God,
Paramatman, Ishwara or whatever you want to call it. So that when this life force is
pleased, it gets purified and merges with the light of the atman.«

»The sugar cane is there, the inside fibrous material is there and the sweetness is the
absolute. Similarly in this case, the final thing is that quality or touch of beingness –
that is the Ishwara principle.
You are that, abide in it and worship that only. Then only will you reach and abide in
the eternal peace; and not by discussing any other precepts regarding spirituality.«

»Q: Somehow I feel responsible for what happens around me.
M: You are responsible only for what you can change. All you can change is your
attitude. There lies your responsibility.«

»V: How about one's livelihood?
Does it happen by itself or does one have to put in an effort to earn one's livelihood?
M: It happens automatically, spontaneously.
Just as you wake up and go to sleep, similarly this also happens.«

»No work is necessary in order to initiate the state of knowledge. But when you are in
a state of knowledge, you can do any work. You must not keep yourself idle; so do go
on working … but when you ask me whether work will help in one's realization, my
answer is that nothing helps there.
Realization is first, then the work starts; duality is lost.«

»Consciousness and life force are two components inextricable woven
together of one principle. But consciousness is only the witnessing principle or the
static aspect; the dynamic aspect or the working principle is the life force.
Once you consider that life force as God itself and that no other God exist, then you
raise the life force to a status enabling it, together with consciousness,
to give you an understanding of the working of the whole principle.«

»What is this vital force and that beingness? They form the quintessence of the
five-elemental play. Being part of it, it has come to frutition as ›I-am-ness‹.
So don't try to make a fragment of it. That quintessential ›I-am-ness‹ means
everything. So when you embrace the body, that ›I-am the body‹ idea, you make a
fragment out of the totality. And this is the crucial mistake.
Whatever experience you get, you study that experience, you understand it,
but who is taking the photographs of all the experiences? Is it the vital breath?
Where do you figure in all this?«

»Now you should find out: How are you going to focus your attention on that vital
breath and meditate on the Self? That is for you to discover.«

»Having understood what the consciousness is and the life force is, I have never gone
to anyone and asked whether my view is correct or incorrect.«

»People have been coming here and I have been talking. Why have I been talking?
Because the life span has to be spent, it has to be used. So even that is
merely entertainment.
Something has to be done; this is entertainment –
whiling away the time, the life span.
The name is the giving of knowledge; but what is the game?
A game of cards, entertainment.
The name is spiritual knowledge; the game is cards.«

Miscellaneous

»The final task in the spiritual quest is to resolve this ultimate distinction;
that between the goal and the path,
between the goal and him who is moving towards it.«
- Sw. Abishiktananda; ›Guru & disciple‹ -

»To the Yogi, body, breath, nerves, mind, prana,
and the universe are all part of a continuum, and he does not set up
artificial distinctions between them.«
- Sw. Rama; ›Science of breath‹, p.83 -

»In Hatha-Yoga for instance, you begin with the bowels and continue to the brain
and beyond. ... Every form of Yoga insists on purity of the body
as a prior condition of superconsciousness.
Every form of Yoga! The books on the subject published
in the west slur over this important matter.
They make concessions to the sloth of their readers,
whose mental as well as physical attitude is well symbolized
by the chocolate-coated pill they swallow to work, while they sleep.
Not so the gurus of the ganges, who insist that there must be activity
within and without – not only awareness of spirit and an eager mind,
but a lively skin and a clean bloodstream –
before you are worthed to stand in the temple of the undistracted mind.«
- F. Yeats-Brown 1937 -

»Purusha in its svarupa is necessarily a non-dual mystery.
All that can be said of it is that it is opposite to Prakriti and conscious,
thus not a doer, totally separate, indifferent, essentially alone.
It sounds simple, but represents unfathomable value and sacred mystery.
Prakriti is equally unmanifest in its root nature,
equally mysterious ... it is also a non-dual mystery.
Its blind inner drive to dynamism, to manifest itself, as it were to show itself
to Purusha, is a many splendored mystery. Completely different in nature,
both uncaused and uncreated, they seem strangely
›made for each other‹ ... the tight dualistic fit in a way prepares the
philosophical ground for advaitic non-dualism.«
- Lloyd W. Pflueger; ›Yoga, the Indian tradition‹, p.76 -

Ramana Maharshi

»Apart from thoughts there is no independent entity called the world.
In deep sleep there are no thoughts and there is no world.
In the states of waking and dream there are thoughts and there is a world also.
Just as a spider emits the thread (of the web) out of itself and again withdraws it into
itself, likewise the mind projects the world out of itself and again resolves it into itself.
When the mind comes out of the Self, the world appears.
Therefore when the world appears (to be real), the Self does not appear;
and when the Self appears (shines) the world does not appear.«
- ›Who am I? Nan Yar‹, ›8‹ –

»Since the Self is the reality of all the gods, the meditation on the Self
which is oneself is the greatest of all meditations«
- ›Vichara Sangraham‹, p.23 -

Avadhuta Gita

»Brahman is neither void nor non-void. It is neither pure nor impure.
It is neither all nor none. Being the selfsame Brahman,
oh mind, why do you weep?« - 5.8 -

»Oh Brahman, by going on a pilgrimage to seek you,
I have denied your omnipresence; by meditating on you,
I have given you form in my mind and thus denied your formless nature;
by singning hymns, I have described you and thus denied your
indescribable nature. Forgive me for these three offenses.« - 8.1 -

»Truly the mind is like space; it seems to face in all directions; it seems to be
everything. But in reality the mind does not exist.« - 1.9 -

Mahavakyas – the great statements:

Prajnanam Brahma: ›Consciousness is Brahma‹ – Aitareya Upanishad (3.1.3) of the
Rig Veda: Lakshana-vakya or the *statement of definition*.

Tat Tvam Asi: ›That thou art‹ – Chandogya Upanishad (6.8.7) of the Sama Veda:
Upadesha-vakya or the *statement of instruction*.

Ayam Atma Brahma: ›This Self is Brahman‹ – Mandukya Upanishad (2) of the
Athara Veda: Abhyasa-vakya or the *statement of practice*.

Aham Brahma Asmi: ›I am Brahman‹ – Brihadaranyaka Upanishad (1.4.10) of the
Yayur Veda: Anubhava-vakya or the *statement of expirience*.